SEEKING A LIVING FAITH

A LENTEN PREACHING SERIES

W. FRANK HARRINGTON

C.S.S. Publishing Co., Inc.

Lima, Ohio

SEEKING A LIVING FAITH

Library of Congress Cataloging-in-Publication Data

Harrington, W. Frank, 1935-
    Seeking a living faith: a Lenten preaching series / W. Frank Harrington
    p.   c.m.
    Includes bibliographies.
    ISBN 1-556-73022-5
    1. Lenten sermons. 2. Sermons, American. 3. Presbyterian Church (U.S.A.) — Sermons. 4. Presbyterian Church — Sermons. I. Title.
BV4277.H315 1988
252'.62—dc19
        87-30932
        CIP

8806 / ISBN 1-55673-022-5

PRINTED IN U.S.A.

Dedicated

to

VICTORIA HARRINGTON FRANCH

and

SUSAN DAWN HARRINGTON

*our daughters, who have taught me about love
and God in special ways.*

Appreciation

(As Paul wrote — "I am a debtor!")

— *To my wife, Sara, and my family whose love and patience sustain me.*

— *To an encouraging congregation who calls forth my best, I do believe that the place is important in the shaping of the preacher.*

— *To my executive assistant, Mrs. Betty Wyatt, whose skills at editing and at the typewriter have been of great value.*

Table of Contents

Introduction

These sermons were inspired by an author who has been an inspiration to me for years. I do not know Maxie Dunnam personally, but I feel I do. I have read all of his books and have been enriched by his sharing of himself. He is a distinguished Methodist clergyman, now serving as Senior Minister of Christ United Methodist Church in Memphis, Tennessee.

Maxie Dunnam's book *Jesus' Claims — Our Promises* made me consider for the first time the "I Am" sayings of Jesus as a unit, as a whole. They speak to life, to the heart of our faith, and significantly they tell us who Jesus is, what he claimed to be. Maxie Dunnam says:

> *In his great "I Am" claims, Jesus is telling us who he is and who God is, He is inviting us to come into his presence, to gaze upon him, to listen to him, to touch him, to receive his love, to accept his forgiveness, to live in him. (p.12)*

Dunnam has written in a devotional context, I have written for proclamation. I commend to you his book, and further study on your part. I have come to believe that the heart of who Jesus is can be found in these statements. They were made in the arenas of life, amid the clash of issues and confrontation. They have an authentic aliveness that challenges — these statements can make a difference in your life and mine. That is why Jesus said what he did — for the same reason I have written these sermons — to make a difference for Christ, in your life, and in mine.

Author's Preface

These sermons on the "I Am" sayings of Jesus are typical of my preaching. The heart of the Church's life is its worship — and central to worship is the proclamation, the preaching of the Word. To understand these sermons you need to know three things about the author. First, preaching is the master passion of my life. I have spent the last twenty-five years in pursuit of effective ideas, telling illustrations, and effective ways to communicate God's full disclosure of himself as revealed in Jesus Christ. Preaching is the foremost task of any minister. It requires disciplined study, life-relatedness, and a willingness to listen both to God and his people.

Secondly, sermons must trace their roots to the Scriptures *and* be rooted in life. Every summer I take two months for study and rest. Prior to that time I pen a letter to the congregation, to people who have written to me in response to our television ministry, and to people I know who are not members of our church. I ask these basic questions:

If you had the responsibility of preaching from the pulpit of the Peachtree Presbyterian Church during the next year, what themes would you consider? What particular truths would you articulate? What needs would you discuss? What issues would you deal with?

The response is tremendous and helpful. I commend it to all who preach! I am also in touch with people — all kinds of people, with all kinds of needs. Contact with people keeps the preacher from answering questions in the pulpit that no one is asking.

It was my privilege to represent the Presbyterian Church at the General Assembly of the Church of Scotland in 1970 and in 1981. During my second visit I met Lord George McLeod, former Moderator of the Church of Scotland, restorer of the Iona Community. Lord McLeod's most famous statement is a reminder to all who preach:

> *I simply argue that the cross be raised again*
> *at the center of the market place*
> *as well as on the steeple of the church,*
> *I am recovering the claim that*
> *Jesus was not crucified in a cathedral*
> *between two candles:*
> *But on a cross between two thieves;*
> *on a town garbage heap;*
> *At a crossroad of politics so cosmopolitan*
> *that they had to write His title*
> *in Hebrew and in Latin and in Greek.*
> *And at the kind of place where cynics talk smut,*
> *and thieves curse and soldiers gamble.*
> *Because that is where He died,*
> *and that is what He died about,*
> *And that is where Christ's men ought to be,*
> *and what the church people ought to be about.*[1]

Finally, above all, I want to be a preacher of hope. I want to be remembered as a preacher of hope, a proclaimer of good news. One of my teachers in graduate school in a conversation after class one day said:

> *Never preach a sermon that does not contain a note of comfort.*

I have never forgotten that, and when I stand to preach I want to bring some light into darkness, some healing into hurts, some wholeness into brokenness, some lift for those who have fallen. I want, I pray always, to be a preacher of hope.

I stand, as do many of you, in a great place, in a great time, for proclamation. Many people have encouraged me. The members of the great church I have served for more than fifteen years have prayed for me and encouraged me to proclaim the Good News. My prayer is that this little volume will bring you hope and encouragement, as well.

[1] Charles R. Swindoll, *Come Before Winter*, (Multnomah Press, Portland, Oregon 1985), p. 207.

W. Frank Harrington
Atlanta, Georgia
January 1, 1987

I Am The Door!

Scripture Reading: John 10:1-10
Text: I am the door; by me if any man enter in He shall be saved, and shall go in and out and find pasture. (John 10:9)

A man born blind had been healed. The Pharisees were incensed about it. They were provoked by the growing acclaim of this Jesus of Nazareth. They were angered that he had dared to heal anyone on the sabbath; it was a breach of their law. So jealous and bothered were they about the success and growing popularity of Jesus, that they could not find it in their hard hearts to rejoice that a man who walked in the darkness of blindness could now see the sunrise and note the twinkle of the stars.

It had to be a trick of some sort, so they began an inquiry:

. . . They interviewed the man's parents to see if, in fact, the man had been blind from birth. His parents, good and decent folks, told the truth — yes, he had been born blind.

. . . They interviewed the man who had been healed and urged him to give God the glory, and deny Jesus as an evil man. The reply of the man who had been healed is worth remembering, "I don't know whether he is good or bad, but this I know I was blind and now I see." (John 9:25)

. . . The Pharisees pressed him about it all — surely there was a hidden agenda somewhere, an angle to all of this widely acclaimed healing and the man simply said, "If this man were not from God, He couldn't do it." (John 9:33)

It was into this context of tension and anger, where those who were the keepers of religious tradition had been such poor shepherds in their caring for the man who was rejoicing in his good fortune, that Jesus picked up on the image of the good shepherd, saying:

> *"I am the door: by me if any man enter in he shall be saved, and shall go in and out and find pasture. (John 10:9)*

It is a statement with profound theological implications. The man had been healed and had been kicked out of the synagogue because he would not cave in to the intense interrogation of the Pharisees. (John 9:34) Our Lord was saying, "They have cast you out, but I have not. They have shut you out, but I reach out for you now. *I am the door*. I welcome you. I invite you."

Ash Wednesday is the beginning of the forty day period of Lent — a time when we prepare for Easter and the glory of the Resurrection. This should be a time of self-examination, confession, and repentance. Edgar A. Guest wrote some words about Ash Wednesday:

> *Time was to church the faithful went,*
> *Repenting every sinful fall.*
> *The priest towards their foreheads bent*
> *And crossed with ashes one and all.*
>
> *This was a symbol to proclaim*
> *The faithful sorrowed for their sins,*
> *From this Ash Wednesday got its name,*
> *The Holy Day when Lent begins.*[1]

So it is appropriate that we focus on this saying of Jesus: "I am the door." The door is the proper symbol, the proper focus, as Lent begins. The door has two functions, to exit or to enter. You can either leave a building, or enter a building by the door. Let's look a bit together at these two functions.

Exit

When you exit, you leave something behind. Someone has said that you never know what is behind a closed door. Behind that door you may leave a house that is cluttered, or a home where strife, anger, and discord are the order of the day. Whatever is behind the door (whether it be joy or sadness), when you exit, you leave it there. At least for a little while, you put something behind you. Or, sometimes when you leave, exit, it is permanent — you cross a threshold in exit never to return again. The closing scene of the famous movie, *Gone With The Wind*, ends with an exit. Rhett Butler is leaving. Scarlett is distraught, and she asks Rhett what will happen to her. You remember his famous reply, "Frankly, my dear, I don't give a damn." He exits, leaving something behind, and according to all reports, he has not returned.

The man whom Jesus had healed had left the old way of blindness behind — now he could see! When they threw him out of the synagogue, Jesus opened a new door for him, and the healed man now left the old way behind. Isn't it true that many of us have things that ought to be left behind — exited, if you please. There are some things we should give up, abandon, exit. It may be a habit that debilitates and destroys. It may be an attitude that makes us less than we ought to be. It may be a relationship that is unworthy — something in the past or in the present.

When he was forty years old, Oscar Hammerstein had worked with thirty different composers. In all that time, nothing jelled, not a single song was successful. To say the least, it was a time of deep discouragement. Finally, Hammerstein met and collaborated with Richard Rodgers, and the following year *Oklahoma* was an enormous success — so great, in fact, that Oscar Hammerstein took a full page ad in *Variety* magazine, with this headline: "I've done it before and I can do it again." He then listed all of his failures.[2]

It is important to acknowledge our failures, to face up to our shortcomings, and then in the grace of Christ, to leave them, to exit. So many of us acknowledge our mistakes and nurse our sins, but we never leave them, nor do we abandon them; we wallow in them and never let them go.

My friend, Dr. Robert Schuller, tells a wonderful story on himself. He was in the midst of a hectic and rushed schedule. He was in New York to deliver a speech and had taken a cab from Manhattan to Long Island. During the ride of about an hour, he was working on his speech and going over his itinerary. He was to be in New York for about three days, and his itinerary was several pages long. As he thought about his speech, he began to make some notes on the back of the itinerary. He was not pleased with his notes, so he tore off a page and crumpled it up, then started to write on the next page of his three day schedule.

Dr. Schuller began to feel better about his speech, and when he arrived at his destination and prepared to leave the cab, he suddenly remembered that the page he had torn out and crumpled up contained his schedule for the next day. He said to the cab driver, who was about to pull away, "Hey, I've got to keep that. I almost threw away part of tomorrow."[3]

Friends, many of us are throwing away our tomorrows because of our inability, our unwillingness, to exit, to leave behind some of those things that keep us from being true to Christ; those things that keep us from being loyal to him so that the royal of his way can come into our lives. Jack Parr put it this way, "My life seems like one long obstacle course, with me as the chief obstacle."

"I am the door," Jesus said. This means that there is an exit, a way to leave behind some things that ought to be forsaken, abandoned, given up. But, it also means that we can:

Enter

A door is not only a way out, an exit, it is also a way in.

Out of the cold weather into the warmth of home, out of the drenching rain into where it is dry, out of fierce wind into where it is calm, out of the danger of being on the outside into the comfort and security of the inside.

When Christ said, "I am the door," within the framework of the *shepherd* image, those who heard him knew immediately what he meant. The sheepfolds that dotted the hills where wandering flocks grazed were "C" shaped. If you were to ask why they had no fixed door or entrance, the shepherd would simply say, "I am the door." At night the shepherd, wrapped in his cloak, would lay down across the entrance. Nothing came in or went out without crossing over or through the shepherd. The shepherd gave security and protection to the sheep by placing himself in the breach of the wall. Our text makes it very clear that those who entered found security, "He shall be saved." They also found new opportunity, "Go in and out and find pasture." Security and opportunity are themes that appeal to us. When we open the door we find security from our sins and opportunity to move on to a more abundant life. The very last sentence in our text reads, "I came that they may have life and may have it abundantly." (John 10:10 [RSV])

New life, abundant life, is the potential of our entering. My family and I were in New York for a few days last summer. There was a particular church I wanted to visit. I had read about the church and wanted very much to see it. Since the church was not far from the hotel where we were staying, I walked down early one morning. When I got there the door was closed and a little sign beside the door read, "Ring the bell and someone will help you."

I rang the bell and nothing happened. No one came, there was no help. I walked around the building and tried several doors; all of them were locked. I began to mutter a bit to myself about "the church of the open door." Why would they put that sign there if it were not true? Finally I came back to where I started and while standing there feeling let down and rejected, another person walked up and rang the bell. Nothing happened, but she did something I had not done — she reached down and tried the latch. And the door opened. It was open all the time and I had not even tried to go in.

Isn't that a parable of your life and mine? There are open doors all around us, just waiting for us to enter, and we never try them, we never open to enter. The most memorable preacher of my childhood was a magnificent figure of a man, Dr. Wells. He had a distinguished educational background and had been president of one of our seminaries. He preached in a swallowtail coat with grey striped trousers, and he ended all of his sermons in the same way, "I have set before you an open door. Will you enter?"

I believe this is the message of Christ to us on Ash Wednesday. The choice is ours. The ball is in our court.

The door is there, it is open, will you enter? We need to accept his invitation and put behind us many experiences of pain that harm and hamper us every day. Some of us cannot make the most of today, or even think of tomorrow, because we are tied to so many yesterdays. It was out of the agony of his betrayal and deceit with another man's wife, deceit that led to murder and the death of the child produced by their adultery, that David cried out:

Create in me a clean heart, O God, and put a new and right spirit within me. Cast me not away from thy presence, and take not thy Holy Spirit from me. Restore to me the joy of thy salvation. — Psalm 51:10-12

I promise you with all of the earnestness of my soul that he can, and he will, restore (to you) to me the joy of salvation. That is what he promised to those who were so captured by the details of religion that they had lost the spirit of caring. He said in the long ago and he says now, "I am the door."

Hast thou no scar?
No hidden scar on foot, or side, or hand?
I hear thee sung a might in the land,
I hear them hail thy bright ascendant star,
Hast thou no scar?

Has thou no wound?
Yet I was wounded by the archers, spent,
Leaned Me against a tree to die; and rent
By ravening beasts that compassed Me, I swooned;
Hast thou no wound?

No wound, no scar?
Yet, as the Master shall the servant be,
And, pierced are the feet that follow Me;
But thine are whole, can he have followed far
Who has no wound nor scar?[4]

Amy Carmichael was right on target when she wrote those words. Tucked away in a quiet corner of every life are wounds and scars. Without them we would need no Christ. With them we have Christ's promise that he is adequate to heal, to forgive. Will you accept that promise?

Notes

[1] Edgar A. Guest, *Ash Wednesday,* From *Lenten-Easter Sourcebook,* edited by Charles L. Wallis, (Abingdon Press, Nashville, TN.: 1961), pp. 27-28.

[2] *Be An Extraordinary Person In An Ordinary World*, edited by Robert A. Schuller, (Fleming H. Revell Company, Old Tappan, New Jersey: 1985), pp. 29-30.

[3] *Ibid*, p.43.

[4] "No Scar," a poem by Amy Carmichael. Copyright material, used by permission of Christian Literature Crusade, Fort Washington, Pennsylvania 1934.

I Am The Good Shepherd!

Scripture Reading: John 10:11-16
Text: *I am the good shepherd. The good shepherd lays down his life for the sheep . . . I know my own sheep and they know me . . . I have other sheep . . . I must bring them also. (John 10:11, 14, 16)*

In 1975, my wife, the girls, and I spent six weeks in Scotland. It was a great time of study and travel, and was one of the most memorable family experiences we have ever had. One of the highlights of the trip occured in the Highlands of Scotland. We encountered a shepherd and his sheep. It was a picture that you would find on a postcard, almost unreal in its beauty and simplicity. The shepherd was dressed in kilts; he was smoking a pipe and carrying a craggy, gnarled, and well-weathered staff in his hand. That morning he was moving 4,000 sheep through the valley. They were moving along slowly, grazing on the sparse grass available. The shepherd was alone assisted by four of those amazing little sheep dogs.

The shepherd was friendly, and took time to visit with us and let us take some pictures. He was very genial, but always alert. He obviously knew when one of his sheep, or groups of them, began to stray. He would call out and, with hand signals, send those little dogs to move the animals back into the main body of the flock. Whenever I think of the Good Shepherd, or whenever I quote the 23rd Psalm — "The Lord is my Shepherd, I shall not want," I think of that pleasant scene from the Highlands of Scotland. The shepherd was strong, alert, and friendly, but his central concern was his sheep.

In the days in which Christ lived, the Middle Eastern shepherd was a wanderer. He had to cover a vast territory to find grazing for his sheep. His work was done in a land that was arid and bleak, and grazing was in short supply. His was a life of eternal vigilance, for there were dangers in that rugged place. His was a life of crushing boredom, for the only thing he had to amuse himself was the task at hand; alone with nothing to distract or stimulate, he had to care for those sheep. In that vast emptiness, with the dangers of their common life, shepherd and sheep became dependent upon one another.

> *The shepherd knew the dependence of his sheep.*
> *He came to know their individuality, he really knew them.*
> *The sheep in their animal limitations, urges and instincts,*
> *trusted and obeyed the shepherd.*[1]

Isaiah put it beautifully when he described what Christ would be in Isaiah 40:11: "He shall feed his flock like a shepherd. He shall gather the lambs with his arms, and carry them in his bosom, and shall gently lead those that are with young."

Small wonder that the image of the *shepherd* was often on the lips of Christ. It was a part of his heritage and culture. Abraham, the father of his nation, was the keeper of great flocks; Moses was tending the flocks of his father-in-law in that desert place when a voice spoke to him from a bush that would not burn and sent him to confront Pharaoh; David was a shepherd boy called in from the fields to be annointed King of Israel. So the image of the shepherd would be very much a part of the heritage of Christ and his culture.

It is this image which he called forth in his confrontation with the Pharisees. He had healed the man who had been born blind. The Pharisees were so concerned about their *legalism* that they could not rejoice in the good fortune of a man who could now see the hopeful glow of the sunrise and the fiery red of the sunset. Jesus told them that they had not been good shepherds. Jesus said to them, "I am the good shepherd."

I think there are four implications of this statement. First of all:

The Good Shepherd Cares For His Sheep!

The text says it in a rather startling fashion, "The hired man runs because he is hired and has no real concern for the sheep." (John 10:13) The key phrase is "no real concern for his sheep." At the first hint of danger, at the first sign of a genuine confrontation, when a vital stand is to be made, only those who care will stand with you. The essential and necessary role of the shepherd is to care for his sheep. Out in the lonely wastes of land near the desert, the dangers were real from brigands, from wild animals. As the shepherd cared for his flock, so Christ, the good shepherd, cares for you and me.

One of the most interesting times in the life of the Peachtree Presbyterian Church during my years as pastor was when the Session of the church engaged in some debate over the new design of our church symbol. Out of that discussion came the crest we now use, and in the heart of that crest, or seal, is the motto: A CHURCH THAT CARES. I believe it was an act of sheer providence that we happened upon that, because it focuses forever on both the mission and the message of the Peachtree Church — that we shall be henceforward and forever *a church that cares*. It focuses on the message that we care because he cared and cares so much for us.

Christ, in his caring, does not promise you or me immunity from suffering, failure, hardships, and hurt from rebellious children, an unhappy marriage, or relationships that do not satisfy. He does promise that he will care for us through all of that and much more. To care is also one of the essential needs and consistent challenges of the human condition.

Maxie Dunnam, in his book *Jesus' Claims — Our Promises*, tells of an interlude of caring. A teenager sent his girlfriend her first orchid corsage and penned this note, "With all my love and most of my allowance."[1]

That reminds me of an incident of several years ago when a distraught young man arrived at our door near midnight. He was in tears, and I asked him to come in. He subsequently spent the night in our home. He and his girlfriend of eighteen months had come to a parting of the ways, and while it might have been *"puppy love"* I can tell you that it was very real to the puppy involved. The next morning, having slept on his anguish, he was somewhat more philosophical and said, "I gave her the best eighteen months of my life and a $35.00 angora sweater!"

We all need to have someone who cares, and we all need to care for someone. The picture of the Good Shepherd as one who cares is, for me, one of the most beautiful and comforting pictures of Christ in the Bible. In his name, we also are to care for each other and for others.

Malcolm Muggeridge wrote very movingly about Mother Teresa after he had seen her work in Calcutta:

> The biggest disease today is not leprosy or tuberculosis, but rather the feeling of being unwanted, uncared for, and deserted by everybody. The greatest evil is the lack of love and charity, the terrible indifference.[2]

To me, one of the best definitions of what it means to care comes from Mother Teresa herself, Calcutta's "Angel of Mercy."

> When I was homeless, you opened your doors,
> When I was naked, you gave me your coat,
>
> When I was weary, you helped me find rest,
> When I was anxious, you calmed all my fears.
>
> When I was little, you taught me to read,
> When I was lonely, you gave me your love,
>
> When in prison, you came to my cell,
> When on sick bed, you cared for my needs.
>
> In a strange country, you made me at home,
> Seeking employment, you found me a job,

Hurt in a battle, you bound up my wounds,
Searching for kindness, you held out your hand.

When I was a Negro, or Chinese or White,
Mocked and insulted, you carried my cross,

When I was aged, you bothered to smile,
When a was restless, you listened and cared.

You saw me covered with spittle and blood,
You knew my features, though grimy with sweat,

When I was laughed at, you stood by my side,
When I was happy, you shared in my joy.[3]

Caring, that is our job! Through good times, through bad times, through boredom, through excitement, and through happiness. It is the one quality all of us need to have and to experience. When Christ said, "I am the good shepherd," he was saying that he cared. He was also saying that:

The Good Shepherd Knows!

Sir George Adam Smith, in an old book, *Historical Geography of the Holy Land*, describes a touching scene by a Judean well. Several flocks of sheep were gathered at the well to be replenished by the water. All of the sheep were intermingled and he wondered how in the world the shepherds would separate the sheep again. But when all of the watering was done and the visiting was over, each shepherd called out in his own unique way and his sheep followed. The flocks went on their separate ways as orderly as they had come. This description gives new meaning to the words of Christ, "I know my own sheep, and they know me." (John 10:15)

Howard Bushnell said that Christ is not the keeper of a hive of bees, knowing well the hive, but not any one bee. Christ is the keeper of a flock, knowing not only the flock, but every sheep in it. It is the hardest thing in the world to grasp, isn't it, how God in all of his almightiness knows each of us by name. And, not only does he know us by name, he knows our needs. He is able to anticipate our needs before we even ask. But, that is why he is God, because he has the capacity to know all of that.[4] This is of great comfort to me, but also a great challenge, for there flash through my mind and heart, as through yours, hurts that wound the heart of God. He knows. He knows, and loves us, not in spite of what he knows, but because of what he knows. He knows us just the way we are, and in the face of that knowledge, he loves us. He finds us where we are and takes us where he wants us to be.

He does not say to those of us who are obese, "I will love you only if you lose weight."

He does not say to those who struggle with being average in school, "If you make the Dean's list I'll love you."

He does not say to the pastor in a small hamlet that is dying, or a village that is on hard times, or the country parish dominated by one family, "I will love you only if you make this church grow and meet its budget." No, he says, "You are *my pastor*, and you love your people, and I will make of you a blessing in their lives."

His love is based on complete knowledge, and it is unlike any love that you can express or I can give. It is complete acceptance in love that knows. It is not a love that condones evil or wickedness, but that challenges us to a new way. It is not a love that is satisfied with what is, but summons us to what can be. It is not a love that capitulates in weakness, but a love of strength that renews and transforms. The Good Shepherd loves us, cares for us, but it is an informed love. He knows.

Some years ago John Callaway interviewed Helen Hayes on public television. You know how these reporters are — they ask a lot of personal, probing questions, which they say is journalism, or the public's right to know. I sometimes think that it is bad manners, but Mrs. Hayes held her composure until he began to zero in on her very stormy marriage to Charles McArthur. Finally, Callaway looked at her and suggested that, with McArthur, she had never known a totally happy day. With great dignity on her face, Hayes said, "Perhaps not a completely happy day, but I knew moments of great ecstasy."[5]

She knew the pain of an inadequate relationship, but she still, God bless her, had the capacity to love. That must be in some small way how God feels about you and about me. He loves us for those moments of glory when we burnish the image that he breathed into us with the breath of life. We must often warm his heart when we do some unselfish thing, but we must also often grieve his spirit with our attitudes and actions, the unloving ways and lack of kindness that seem to characterize our lives. But, nothing takes away his capacity to care and to know.

The good shepherd not only cares and knows, but:

The Good Shepherd Protects!

The text puts it this way, "The good shepherd lays down his life for the sheep." (John 10:11)

There was danger out in the desert wastelands as they searched for the sparse strips of grass. There was danger from wild beasts and unprincipled men. Human greed is not confined to the streets of a city, it raises its ugly head wherever humankind makes its way.

The good shepherd must be prepared to sacrifice, to lay down his life for his sheep in some sudden confrontation. Again, I refer to the observations of Sir George Adam Smith. He said that he never saw a flock of sheep without a shepherd.

On some high moor — across which at night the hyenas howl — when you meet him, sleepless, far-sighted, weatherbeaten, armed, leaning on his staff and looking out over his scattered sheep, every one of them on his heart.

Out there in the desert in the bone chilling cold of the night and the strength sapping heat of the day, the shepherd must always be prepared to sacrifice, if necessary, for his sheep. In the Cathedral of Notre Dame in Paris, there is a window in memory of an Archbishop who was killed in one of the many political upheavals in that city. Underneath the window in the sacristy there is this inscription, "The good shepherd giveth his life for the sheep."[6]

If you look around, you can see that kind of love operative today. A physician friend of mine recently made a sacrifice for one of his children. He gave one of his kidneys that his daughter might have a chance at life. Many of us know stories of parents who protected their children, placing themselves between the child and the danger. This is the spirit of the good shepherd as he protects.

Do you know the gospel songwriter, Stuart Hamblen? He put it so powerfully in his song "He Bought My Soul":

Each drop of blood bought me a million years;
A soul was born each time he shed a tear;
He loosed the chains that fetter you and me;
He bought my soul from death at calvary.[7]

"I am the good shepherd," Jesus said, and the good shepherd cares, knows, protects, and:

The Good Shepherd's Love Is Not Narrow!

The Pharisees believed they had the exclusive right on the franchise of God's love. Christ said, not so, "I have other sheep, too, in another fold. I must bring them also." (John 10:16)

He threw the guantlet down at their feet. There is no narrowness or exclusivity in the heart of God. This is the mandate of the church, to be constantly reaching out, seeking, wooing, winning, trying to find those other sheep.

O tender Shepherd climbing rugged mountains
    and crossing waters deep —
How long would'st thou be willing to go homeless
To find a straying sheep?
I count no time, the Shepherd gently answered,
As thou dost count and bind
The weeks in months, the months in years,
My counting is just — until I find.
And that would be the limit of My journey
I'd cross the waters deep,
And climb the hillsides with unfailing patience
Until I find My sheep.[8]

There is nothing narrow or exclusive about the role of the good shepherd. It is certainly wider than the walls of any church. The good shepherd must be always seeking, searching, and trying to find the sheep that need care. The good shepherd knows, cares, protects, and his love is not narrow.

La Mesa Penitentiary in Tiajuana, Mexico is a grim and harsh place. It is the end of the line for those incarcerated there. Behind those prison walls there is a person who never committed a crime, never robbed or murdered anyone, and at no time engaged in illegal activity. Everyone in the prison knows the innocence of the person.

That person takes three meals a day with the prisoners, eats what they eat, where they eat, sleeps in a cell, follows the same schedule, and is awakened every morning by a guard. Her name is Sister Antonia Brenner, a native of California, who insists that her stay there is her calling. The prisoners at La Mesa call her "the white angel." Sister Antonia calls herself a "prisoner of love." If a prisoner has a family member ill or in trouble, she leaves the prison to visit that person and comes back to inform and to reassure. If a relative of a prisoner dies, she attends the funeral so that she can describe to the inmate what happened, who was there, and bring comfort and news of the family. She responds to a great variety of personal needs, from securing a comb, to finding a lawyer, or just being a friend.

She does not hesitate to give herself in friendship, and is seen patting the prisoners on the back and, occasionally, hugging one of them. Some people consider her role there to be the product of naivete and dangerous, but none of that deters her from committing herself more completely to her ministry behind those prison walls.

On one occasion when she was being criticized for her work, she took out a white napkin and put a black dot in the middle of it. She asked the person who had confronted her, "What do you see?" He obviously saw only the black dot, and then she added, "With the men here, most outsiders see only that they are murderers or thieves. They don't see the rest of them. I do. Yes, I see the bad in people, but I also see the good."[9]

Truly, Sister Antonia's love is not narrow.

I remember, as a watershed moment in my life, the day I learned that I had the capacity to be a good shepherd. It takes tough love to be a good shepherd. It has to be tough when you are called on to love someone who has been actively hostile, a constant critic, a thorn in the flesh; someone who has actively, publicly opposed most of what you stood for. About 2:30 one morning the phone rang; little Bill was near death from a wreck. I immediately dressed and went to the University Hospital, and as I drove there I thought what an unusual providence it was that prompted me as the pastor to go to this family.

The parents and grandparents of this boy had done everything they could to be a barrier to my ministry. They had never supported the church in general and were hostile to me in particular. As a matter of fact, they had surreptitiously approached members of the Session about firing me. But, now they needed me. There we were standing in the darkened corridors of the hospital, their son fighting for his life. I spoke to them, and reached out and hugged them, then went into the intensive care unit. When I saw the boy, I knew that if he lived, his life would be drastically limited. But, I also knew in that moment that whatever our differences might be, their need, in Christ's name, was bigger than that difference. For several days I stayed with that family, night and day. They were comforted by my presence, though I could tell they felt a bit awkward about the past. Little Bill died, and I conducted his funeral.

I discovered something about myself that day that has stood me in good stead all these years. I was their shepherd and they needed me, and for me that was bigger than differences of personalities or hostility. I can tell you that, by the grace of God, I have always been able to be a good shepherd, whatever the need, whoever the person, whatever the circumstance.

There are some things deeper than our hurts, bigger than our peculiarities, larger than our differences, and in Christ's name, being a good shepherd is one of them. God has given each of us an opportunity to be good shepherds to many.

To be a good shepherd is:

To see value that is not obvious,
To find the wanderer who is lost,
To make things strong so that they can last,
To cultivate deep roots that can sustain,
To be a light in darkness,
To renew those who are broken
To make something royal in the ruts of the common way!

That is your task and mine, for we are called to be a good shepherd to somebody. It is my prayer that the image of the Good Shepherd who cares, who knows, who protects, and whose love is without limits will be burned into our hearts, and that we will seek to fashion our lives after that image.

Notes

[1] Maxie Dunnam, *Jesus' Claims — Our Promises*, (The Upper Room, Nashville, Tennessee, 1985), p. 37.

[2] Malcolm Muggeridge, *Something Beautiful For God*, (Ballentine Books, New York, New York 1971), p. 55.

[3] *Ibid*, p. 58

[4] Charles R. Swindoll, *Come Before Winter*, (Multnomah Press, Portland, Oregon, 1985), p. 204.

[5] Leo Buscaglia, *Loving Each Other*, (Slack Incorporated, Thorofare, New Jersey, 1984), p. 17.

[6] *The Gospel According to St. John*, Volume I, The Speaker's Bible, edited by James and Edward Hastings. (Baker Book House, Grand Rapids, Michigan, 1962), pp. 223-224.

[7] "He Bought My Soul" by Stuart Hamblen, Copyright © 1949 by Hamblen Music Company. Copyright Renewed. All Rights Administered by Unichappell Music, Inc. International Copyright Secured. All rights reserved. Used by permission.

[8] *Gospel of St. John*, Volume I, Speaker's Bible, p. 223

[9] Ted Engstrom, *The Fine Art of Friendship*, (Thomas Nelson Publishers, Nashville, Tennessee, 1985), pp. 127-128.

I Am The Bread Of Life!

Scripture Reading: John 6:35-40
Text: Jesus said to them, "I am the bread of life; he who comes to me shall not hunger, and he who believes in me shall never die."
(John 6:35)

Jesus had just fed 5,000 people with five barley loaves and two fish, which a lad had stepped forward and offered to the hungry people. The crowd was electrified by the miracle, and pressed upon Jesus. He must be the leader they were looking for, the one who could make things better for them. They surged forward to be with him, and Jesus withdrew into the mountains alone.

The next morning they were waiting for him, but they had bread on their minds. They wanted more miracles! I can tell you that anyone promising *bread* for everybody can draw a crowd almost anywhere in the world today. Bread sustains life. It is needed for life. Political leaders rise and fall on the question of bread. The world still ponders how the madman, Hitler, came to power in Germany — a people of culture, education, art and religion. He came to power on the question of *bread*. The German economy was in shambles, the great war preparations were drawing away their capacity to meet the basic needs of people. And on the rising tide of frustration concerning bread, Hitler came to power. From time to time you get a glimpse of what life is really like in the Soviet Union. The editorial writers talk about a lack of consumer goods for the people. They have to stand in line to get the basic necessities of life in that society, and there must be concern in the inner workings of the Soviet government over the question of bread.

In this nation in elections, large and small, we frequently hear that the issue is *economy*. The real question is bread. Will I have enough money to buy the things that are needed for life, or will the staggering, faltering economy deprive me of my capacity to provide bread for the folks I love the most? By the Sea of Galilee in the long ago, Jesus was dealing with one of life's basic questions — the question of *bread*! He dealt with it in such a dramatic fashion that the crowd was electrified. He took a little and made a lot, and everyone had enough to eat and more. It is the kind of thing that draws a crowd in any society, at any time.

Let us note that:

The Hunger Of This World Is Real

The physical hunger that stalks this world is real, and it grows worse with every passing day. No one really has a handle on it. We do what we can, but still the vacant eyes and the bloated bellies of little children stare at us from our television sets. We sit in our abundance and try to relate to the horror of places where there is no bread.

Some of the hunger is caused by political systems that are insensitive at best, or capricious in their intentions at worst. The present population of the world is 4 billion. The experts tell us that it will double to 8 billion in less than 40 years, and will probably stabilize, we hope, at about 11 billion.[1] This means that the demand for food is growing and the supply of food is shrinking. More than 10,000 people starve to death in this world of ours every day.[2] The question of bread is much with us, it is real, it is urgent.

Do you remember the nursery rhyme:

There was an old woman who lived in a shoe,
She had so many children she didn't know what to do;
She gave them some broth without any bread,
She whipped them all soundly and put them to bed.[3]

There are many of God's children who will go to bed tonight without any bread, and with little hope of ever having enough.

The hunger of this world is real, make no mistake about it. But there is another hunger that Jesus talked about that day as he responded to the crowd crying out for more bread, more miracles. He said to them, "I am the bread of life; he who comes to me shall not hunger, and he who believes in me shall never die."

In Matthew's Gospel, the fourth chapter, verse six we find these words, "Man shall not live by bread alone."

Even if the stomach is filled with a sufficiency, this is not all that life requires. There is a hunger, a gnawing hunger of the spirit that must be filled. Man lives by truth, by wonder, by worship. These hungers must be satisfied. Jesus was using the crowd's reaction to the obvious to teach them, and to teach us a deeper truth. There is a hunger of the heart that must be filled.

Some poet has written:

Not only by bread man lives, but by
  Awe and delight and wonder still,
By glory of the sea and sky,
  And mystery of the purple hill.[4]
                                    — *Katherine Tynan*

Mohammed, the prophet of Islam, came close to what I am saying when he wrote, "If thou hast two loaves, sell one and buy lilies."

We need more than bread to really satisfy ourselves, for there is a hunger in you and in me that mere bread will not fully satisfy.

When Shakleton, the explorer, lost his ship "Endurance" in the Antarctic, and prepared his men for an arduous journey to safety, he told them they must travel light. They must throw away everything and anything that was not needed to sustain life. He tells us that only with reluctance did they keep the bread which might be the difference between life and death in a few days. Money was of no value at all and was heavy to carry. The one thing they preserved to the end were private photographs of home folks, pictures of children, wife, family, parents. It was food for their souls, a stimulus and strength for an arduous journey. This is how Shakleton described it, "Sovereigns were thrown away, photographs were kept."[5]

The hunger of this world is real. There is a physical hunger that stalks the earth for many. Many who hunger for bread live with little hope that this need will ever be met. But "man shall not live by bread alone." There is a deeper hunger of the heart, just as vital, just as crucial. Life depends on two kinds of bread, *real* and *spiritual*. Christ is committed, his church is committed, to meeting both of these hungers.

The Response Of Christianity To Both Hungers Is To Share!

Everything is based on sharing. If some were not farmers, millers, or makers of bread all of the time, then all of us would have to be farmers and millers part of the time. We are interdependent upon one another. The Christian response to *real* hunger and *spiritual* hunger is to share. We share our bread and we share our Christ.

We must share what we have so that others might live. Or, as someone has phrased it, "we must learn to live more simply so that some might simply live." So often this sharing of our substance, *real bread*, must come first. If people are so hungry for food that they cannot see straight, this reality dominates their lives. They cannot hear our words about Christ, because the rumbles of the stomach drown out the sounds of our holy words.

We must learn how to share. Meister Eckhart said in one of his messages:

As long as you are more concerned for yourself than you are for people you have never seen, you are wrong and you cannot have an even momentary insight into the simple care of the soul.[6]

At present, the United States, with one fifteenth of the

world's population, uses well over half of all the raw materials consumed each year. Let's face it, the people of this earth, in mounting animosity, will not allow us to continue on this track. We must — we must in humility and compassion — learn how to share our abundance with others.

While we share our abundance to meet the needs of *real* hunger, we must also share our Christ to meet *spiritual* hunger. D. T. Niles said that evangelism is one beggar telling another where to find bread. That is the spirit in which the church goes forth to evangelize, to woo, to win for Christ. When G. J. Romanes died in 1894 he left some notes, and they were published after his death. Among those posthumous notes we find these words, "There is a vacuum in the soul of man which nothing can fill save faith in God."[7]

Distinguished scientist, serious banker, classroom teacher, village mechanic, parish priest, or neighborhood paper boy, there is a vacuum in every heart that can only be filled by God. We must share our Christ.

A well dressed man of business called and asked to meet with me in late afternoon. I liked the cut of the man. His vocabulary would indicate that he had been well educated, for he demonstrated a good choice of words and a wide ranging use of words. He indicated that he had been watching our television services and had been drawn to the sermons and the service of worship.

He then, with a mounting urgency in his voice said, "Let's face it. I've got everything that money can buy, but I sense, I know, that something is missing in my life. When I hear you preach I know that you have something that I do not have and I want it."

As gently as I could, I told him that I was not at all sure that I had all he thought I had, but I would share all that I knew, and all that I have experienced of Christ, with him. He had solved one of the basic hungers, he had all of the *bread* he needed, but he needed something more.

A beautiful young lady, whom I watched grow up, has

come upon hard times. In total rebellion against her parents now for some two or three years, her life has been and is the nightmare that we pray will never befall any of our children. She has had a series of lovers, here today and gone tomorrow — at least two abortions along the way. A stormy marriage with periodic beatings — she is caught in a cycle of abuse and need that drives her to despair. She cannot live with herself, or her husband. Her parents are caught between distress and anger. Something basic drifted to the surface recently, and this young woman called me. Her opening statement to me was, "What is going to happen to me? I want to get my life straightened out. What is missing in my life?"

I can tell you — it is a deep, inner hunger that must be satisfied. I believe that only the love of God, experienced in her soul, will lift her up out of a path of destruction. There is a hunger gnawing away at her that only God can satisfy.

Dollars, status, and security have an insatiable appetite that can never be satisfied, nor will it ever fully satisfy you and me. I do not care how big a bulge there is in your stock portfolio, how much land you own, how many C.D.'s you have on deposit. I can tell you that in the final analysis, when the dust settles on all of life, these things will not, and cannot, satisfy.

A dear member of my church was awaiting the final roll call. I went to see him just twenty-four hours before he died. He was weak, but alert, serene and unafraid. Surrounded by a loving family his chief concern was for them. He asked them to leave so we could talk. I held his hand, and this is what he said to me:

I am awaiting my final promotion, the moment which all of life has been but preparation. I want you to know that I am ready, grieve not for me, but look after my family for me when I am gone.

I promised him I would, and I have. There was no hunger in his heart for God, he was ready, and his concern was not for self, but for others.

Senator Mark Hatfield once said to Mother Teresa, "How can you go out on the streets of Calcutta, day after day, to minister to the sick and dying, when you can never meet the need?" She answered, "The Lord does not call us to be successful, He calls us to be faithful."[8]

When Jesus said, "I am the bread of life," he said something basic. He knew that the hungers of this world, *physically* and *spiritually*, are real. He showed us the way to meet both hungers by sharing our material substance, and by sharing our Christ with all who will listen.

But there is more:

The Primary Focus of Your Life and Mine Should Be on Satisfying the Spiritual Hunger That Gnaws at Our Innermost Being!

In many places, time and time again, our Lord centers on this *spiritual* hunger. In our text he says, "No one coming to me will ever be hungry again." In Matthew's Gospel he said, "Man shall not live by bread alone." (Matthew 4:4) And in Matthew 6:33 we find these words, "Seek ye first the kingdom of God and his righteousness, and these other things will be added unto you."

Bread as it is used here is symbolic. It represents all the technology, all of the material goods, the abundance that is ours, all of the conveniences and gadgets, all of the entertainment and the arts, all of the things that make life beautiful and good. He is saying to you and to me that life is bigger than all of that. There is a powerful temptation in life to think that this bread is enough. Let's face it, most of our energies are spent on "the bread that cannot fully satisfy."

We have more than we need of the things we can taste, feel, hear, touch, see, and smell. We are a violent society. Crime is rearing its ugly head at every level — there is a rampant breakdown of the American family. What happiness has all this bread brought us?

The hunger that stalks your life and mine is a deeper hunger that the heart knows, but the eyes cannot see. The hands cannot touch it, the tongue cannot taste it, the nose cannot smell it, and ears cannot hear it. There is a deeper hunger in us that must be satisfied if we are to be all that God meant for us, and wants us to be.

That deeper hunger is seen in teaching our children how to walk, but giving no direction as to where to walk.

That deeper hunger is seen in teaching our children how to read, but giving no direction as to what they should read.

We are talking about focus — about priorities. When life has that proper focus and the deeper hunger is met, then life will give us in abundance three things:

1. *A sense of satisfaction.* A sense of well-being. Some years ago a woman was admitted to a hospital for treatment. After being a patient for three months, she asked for a larger room, a large canvas, and lots of paints. Every request was granted, for they were trying to help her find herself.

Six months later she invited the administrator of the hospital and members of the nursing staff to her room to see her painting. She spoke of it as her life's work, and after everyone was seated, she unveiled with a dramatic flourish her masterpiece. It was a shock! Everyone was stunned, for the canvas was completely white, not a stroke had been made, not a dot of paint stained the canvas.

No one knew quite what to do, so they just sat staring at the canvas. Finally the administrator asked her, "What is it?" She responded with great enthusiasm, "It's the children of Israel crossing the Red Sea."

Everyone just looked puzzled and the administrator asked a second question, "Where is the Red Sea?" Her answer was grounded in perfect logic for her, "The Red Sea has parted! Half is on one side of the canvas and half on the other." Then said the administrator, "Where are the children of Israel?" "Oh," said the artist, "they have already gone through."

The administrator was about out of questions, but he still had one more, "Where is Pharaoh and the Egyptian Army?" Her reply was to the point, "Oh, they haven't arrived yet!"[9]

The sheer pathos of that story is staggering — what a shame it is or would be, to live your life and not make a mark. To live a life that is a blank canvas. I can tell you this, that if the focus of life is right — if the hunger of the heart that longs for God is satisfied — there will be a sense of satisfaction in that life, and the "peace that passes all human understanding."

2. *There is a larger purpose* that takes hold of your life and mine. We are called upon to meet the actual hungers of friend and neighbor, but also to touch that deeper hunger of friend and neighbor's heart. Ours is a life of giving rather than getting, of sharing and reaching out rather than grasping and holding to ourselves. Albert Schweitzer not only taught us by what he wrote, he taught us by what he was. He didn't just talk about Africa and all its needs, he went there and devoted his life to helping others. He said:

> It is not enough merely to exist. It is not enough to say, "I'm earning enough to live and to support my family. I do my work well, I'm a good father. I'm a good husband. I'm a good churchgoer." That's all very well. But you must do something more. Seek always to do some good somewhere. Every man has to seek in his own way to make his own self more noble and to realize his own true worth. You must give some time to your fellowman.

When we eat of the bread that Christ came to give us, we shall not only have a sense of satisfaction in life, we shall be motivated by a larger purpose, and,

3. *We shall experience an abiding certainty*. Look again at our text, "No one coming to me will ever be hungry again." There should be a sense of certainty about our faith. It might come soon for some, late for others, but it should come. If you don't

have it don't give up, keep going, work hard, keep the faith, for Jesus promised us that he is "the bread of life," and that no one coming to him will ever be hungry again.

There is a remarkable story about the Chinese bamboo tree. The Chinese plant the seed, water it, fertilize it, but during the first year nothing happens. The second year they water and fertilize it, and nothing happens. The third year, the fourth year, they water and fertilize it, and nothing happens. Then, in the fifth year, after about four and a half years of watering and fertilizing and watching the ground where the seed was planted, and seeing nothing — the bamboo tree shoots up out of the earth and grows ninety feet in six weeks.

The question is this: Did it grow ninety feet in six weeks, or in five years? The answer is five years, because if they had not applied water and fertilizer every year for five years, there would have been no bamboo tree.[10]

We are all like that tree, we must work hard, apply the faith, respond to the opportunities God gives us, and then — then — by the grace of God, we will come to know an abiding sense of certainty. Then we shall experience what the hymnwriter set to music:

> Drop thy still dews of quietness, till all our
>   strivings cease,
> And let our ordered lives confess the beauty of
>   thy peace.
> — *John Greenleaf Whittier*

In the long ago Jesus told a crowd pressed around him, "I am the Bread of life. No one coming to me will ever be hungry again." How thankful we should be for this precious promise of our Lord.

Notes

[1] *TIME MAGAZINE*, "How to Defuse the Population Bomb," October 24, 1977.

[2] Paul R. Erlich, *The Population Bomb*, (Ballentine Books, New York, 1968), pp. 25-26.

[3] Tim Timmons, *Maximum Living In A Pressure Cooker World*, (Word Books, Waco, Texas, 1979), p. 29.

[4] Poem by Katherine Tynan, *The Gospel According to St. Matthew*, The Speaker's Bible, Volume I, (Baker Book House, Grand Rapids, Michigan, 1963), p. 66.

[5] *Ibid*, p. 66

[6] Maxie Dunnam, *Jesus's Claims — Our Promises*, (The Upper Room, Nashville, Tennessee, 1985), p. 22.

[7] *The Gospel According to St. John*, Volume I, The Speaker's Bible, (Baker Book House, Grand Rapids, Michigan, 1962), p. 149.

[8] David L. McKenna, *Renewing Our Ministry*, (Word Books, Waco, Texas, 1986), p. 128.

[9] Tim Timmons and Stephen Arterburn, *Hooked On Life,* (Oliver Nelson, Nashville, Tennessee, 1985) pp. 212-213.

[10] Zig Ziglar, *Raising Positive Kids in a Negative World, (Oliver Nelson, Nashville, Tennessee, 1985), p. 225.*

I Am The Vine!

Scripture Reading: John 15:1-8
Text: I am the vine, you are the branches. (John 15:5)

Our Lord's teaching on the *vine* and the *branches* came immediately after the Last Supper. The evening was over, the table talk was done. The betrayer had gone out into the darkness to do his dastardly deed. Peter was left with his thoughts on the coming prediction of denial. The ambitions of the disciples were still there, but the evening hour was over. The final statement of Chapter 14 in the Gospel of John indicates that it was over, for Jesus said, "Come, let's be going." (John 14:31 [TBL])

This means, then, that the teachings concerning the *vine* and the *branches* took place somewhere along the way between the Upper Room and Gethsemane. They would be walking about a mile from the place where they had enjoyed a meal together:

> *Past the fountain of Siloam, out of the water gate, turning to the left up the Valley of Kidron, past the priestly tombs, under the great mass of the temple — to the Garden of Gethsemane.*[1]

It was during the season when vines were being trimmed in the gardens nearby. As work was done on pruning the limbs, debris was thrown into the street to wither, and would eventually be burned. I can well imagine that as they walked along talking, they were stepping over or walking by some of the prunings, and could actually see that they had been recently cut from the vines. Jesus did, then, what he often did — he took some familiar thing and taught a powerful lesson.

He had been telling them that the time would soon come when he would no longer be physically able to walk, talk, and have fellowship with them. He knew that the confrontation between his followers and the powerful interests of religion and state would continue when he was gone. Many of them would be thrown out of their synagogues and would be threatened. He was suggesting in a powerful way, that there is no life, no vitality, apart from him. So Jesus said to them, "I am the vine, you are the branches."

He was saying to them, "I am the most vital connection of them all." If you are to be all that I want you to be, you must remember that "I am the vine" — the source of life, sustenance, and strength. If you are to be a fruit bearing branch, then you must remember the source of all your power.

Some poet has captured this thought:

> *Every virtue we possess,*
> *And every victory won,*
> *And every thought of holiness,*
> *Are His alone.*

Christ is the source, the essence of all that we are as Christians. Christ is the focus, the force, the power of our faith.

Maxie Dunnam, former editor of *The Upper Room* and a distinguished Methodist clergyman, says that this text centers on three words: *abide*, *apart*, and *ask*.

Abide

This word occurs ten times in the first eleven verses of John 15. "Abide in me, and I in you. As the branch cannot bear fruit by itself, unless it abides in the vine, neither can you, unless you abide in me." (John 15:4) *The Living Bible* paraphrases this in a very appealing way, "Take care to live in me, and let me live in you." (John 15:4)

Again and again, the Bible speaks of this vital connection. Paul said, "It is not I who lives, but Christ who lives within me." "For me to live is Christ." "I can do all things through Christ who gives me inward power."

As John uses it, the word *abide* has a powerful message. It speaks not so much of a place, a place to stay, to dwell, but of a relationship. Christ can be with us, in us, directing us, helping us, guiding us, anywhere, anyplace, anytime. Maxie Dunnam says that abiding in Christ means, "At least three things: realizing His presence, responding to His prodding and probing, and resting in His peace."[2]

There is nothing passive about abiding in Christ. If we are relating to him, this is going to be anything but passive. We are going to give ourselves to something, to someone. God made us that way. Let's look at two quotations. Dr. Menninger onced asked a very wealthy patient, "What on earth are you going to do with all that money?"

The patient in response said, "Just worry about it, I suppose."

Pressing the question a bit, Dr. Menninger asked, "Well, do you get that much pleasure out of worrying about it?"

The response of the patient is sobering, "No, but I get such terror when I think of giving some of it to somebody."[3]

Isn't that sad? With all of that capacity to be and to do, — being so totally immobilized by the inability to share, to give, to look beyond himself.

I was told a story about the time a rather well-known Atlanta businessman of a generation ago died. His family gathered in one of the downtown law firms to hear the reading of his will. It began with this phrase, "Being of sane mind, I spent it all."

Dietrich Bonnoeffer rightly observed that, "Our hearts have room only for one all-embracing devotion, and we can only cleave to one Lord."[4]

If we are to abide in Christ, it speaks of a relationship with him. A relationship which responds to his nearness, responds to his teaching, and claims the abundance of life that he promises. We are so often caught up in the busyness of life, in what we are doing, desiring, debating, that we forget we need a higher connection to realize all that God wants for your life and mine. We tend to compartmentalize our religion for Sunday at church, and then forget about it in the world of reality — where the issues of life are joined and where faith needs to be operative.

A young man came to see me about a rather thorny decision he had to make. It involved a question of ethics. He was a stockbroker, and by all standards of measurement was doing well, but something had come up. I listened as he shared his concerns with me, and I finally said to him, "What does your faith say to you in this situation?" He gave me the strangest of looks — a look of utter surprise, and very bluntly he said, "What does faith have to do with this? This is business."

We need in life, in business, a higher connection. We need a relationship with Christ; and all of this is implied in the word *abide*. For twenty-six years now, I have been a minister. I struggle to live what I preach. I seek in public proclamation and private devotion to respond to Christ's way. I have never been and never will be a perfect example of Christian living. But, I am striving to do better, to be better. After spending half of my life as a minister, I have come to the conclusion that all of us have four choices regarding Jesus Christ.

1. We can hear and reject.

2. We can hear and give lip service. We can go through the motions of responding to Christ. As someone has said, "having enough religion to make ourself miserable." Many people that we all know and love are caught up in this basic pretense. Their names are on the roles of some church. They rarely attend, they give little support, they are the makers of excuses — it is never the right time to give, to serve, to support, to actively engage in the Master's business.

3. We can hear and make a partial commitment. Some people go so far, and no further. The commitment is

not total. Many of these folk are somewhat active in church, and have a tendency to be critical of those who serve and work. They are sometimes hung up on "the church that used to be," how things "once were." Others are growing and they are left by the way. I think Augustine spoke for many of them when he cried out in his prayers, "Lord, make me a new man, but not yet."

4. We can hear and accept, *abide* in our relationship with Christ. This is the foundation of our Christian pilgrimage. It is out of this commitment that we find new life in Christ. There is no other way.

I was recently listening to one of the T.V. preachers and he asked a rhetorical question in his sermon: "What does it cost to join this church?" Then, with a flourish he answered, "Nothing!" I challenge that statement today. It is very costly to accept Christ and to join a church. It is costly not in terms of dollars, but in terms of commitment. We expect the members of Peachtree Presbyterian Church to be serious about what Christ means in their life. If he is vitally connected to your life in a serious way, then you are going to be living in a manner worthy of his name. You are going to be giving generously of your finances, standing tall, serving with eagerness, and you are going to be regularly in the house of God for worship. If any of those elements are missing — then something is awry in your commitment.

If Christ is vitally connected to your life and mine, we should not always be debating the question, "What is my share?" What is my share of the building fund, the teaching ministry, the service and nuture ministries of the church. But our lives should flow out of a bedrock commitment that says all that is mine is God's, and I share it freely. There is nothing cheap about the grace of God that is available through his church. He should be first in your life. It is a reality that if your worship attendance is spotty, if your giving is not commensurate with your means to give, if your service is given grudgingly, and if your life is just marginally what Christ expects — then your spiritual life is in trouble. We are to *abide* in him, and that means relate to him completely; nothing else is sufficient, nothing else will do.

Perhaps this illustration will say it better. Yonder in Westminster Abbey, there is the tomb of Christopher Chapman. The date is 1680 and the inscription reads, "What I gave I have. What I spent I had. What I left I lost by not giving it."[5]

To abide in Christ, the vine, the flow of life is reversed, it flows outward, not inward on self, but outward expressing the love of Jesus Christ. Always, everywhere, every day, every place, for every person, the flow is outward.

I'll go where you want me to go, dear Lord.
Real service is what I desire.
I'll say what you want me to say, dear Lord,
But don't ask me to sing in the choir!

I'll say what you want me to say, dear Lord.
I like to see things come to pass,
But don't ask me to teach girls and boys, dear Lord,
I just want to stay in my class.

I'll do what you want me to do, dear Lord;
I yearn for the Kingdom to thrive;
I'll give you my nickles and dimes, dear Lord,
But please don't ask me to tithe.

I'll go where you want me to go, dear Lord;
I'll say what you want me to say:
I'm busy just now with myself, dear Lord,
I'll help you some other day.
                                        — Sabido

If you are abiding in him, you are going to be hearing the

drum beats of a drummer that says the flow of life is outward. You are going to want to be involved in helping others, you won't have to be coerced because you are abiding in him!

The second great word is:

Apart!

Christ said, "Apart from me you can do nothing." (John 15:5) *The Living Bible* is helpful again, "Apart from me you can't do a thing."

Apart from Christ, the vital connection is broken. It is like unplugging a lamp; the source of power is denied, no light is available. A friendship will deteriorate and die if there is no contact. A marriage will not flourish without some togetherness. A vocational relationship will end if you do not show up for work. A vital church relationship will die if there is no active participation and involvement. Anything that is valuable — that grows — that is alive and healthy — depends on a vital connection, on contact. The same is true in our faith. We cannot stand *apart* without connection, and expect anything to happen. There is no life in our faith apart from Christ.

That is a hard thing for us to accept. We were brought up on the philosophy of *rugged individualism*. It is the American dream — to take initiative, work hard, and success will be ours. We all like to think of ourselves as being self-made. There is no such thing as a self-made man or woman. All of us stand on the shoulders of those who came before us, and we owe a great debt of gratitude to them.

I was introduced the other day by a friend who called me a "self-made man." He referred to the fact that I worked my way through Presbyterian College. Nothing could be further from the truth. All along life's way, at important times, some person reached out to me to help. It began with my parents who encouraged and loved me; it continued through the friendship of Christian ministers distinguished in their own rights, who had no reason whatever to reach out to me, but did. My wife, Sara, for more than thirty-one years has served with me — and I can assure you that I could not be the minister I've been without her strong support and encouragement.

For fifteen years I have been encouraged by the people of the Peachtree Presbyterian Church to walk into the pulpit and to dream great dreams. I am not self-made, nor are you. None of us stand alone. But this rugged individualism concept dies hard. I think of the *Challenger* disaster; the explosion of that shuttle was a shaking and sobering event for us. It had all become so routine. We believe our technology is omnipotent — from instantaneous communication to test tube babies. And then that rocket, soaring upward with an orange plume sending it on, a searing moment of fire in the sky; it caused many to remember, "Apart from me you can do nothing."

There is no individualized religion, no bootstrap faith. Hundreds of years before we were even alive, Seneca, the Roman poet, said:

> *I have been trying to climb out of the pit of my besetting sins . . . in vain. And I never can, and never will, unless a hand is let down to me to draw me up . . . The Gods are not jealous. If a man will climb up eagerly they stretch out a hand to him.*[6]

Apart from God we can do nothing. A famous explorer was making his way through the region of the upper Amazon. They were compelled, because of conditions, to make a forced march two days in succession. On the morning of the third day, he found all his native carriers prostrate on the ground, and they would not move. They were asked to get going, and finally their spokesman said, "They are waiting. They cannot move till their souls have caught up with their bodies."[7] I love that story. We all need that vital connection of mind, body, and spirit! It just may be that the reason that our faith is so timid, that our sense of purpose in life is so obscure, that we are unable to find our niche, is because we are apart. We are lacking the connection that sustains. One of the most comforting passages in the New Testament is that word from Paul, "Nothing can separate us from the love of Christ."

But there is something that can separate us from knowing the love of Christ. By a deliberate act of will, or by the indifference of benign neglect, we can be lost and separated from his love.

Three key words tell the story of this text: *Abide* speaks of a relationship with Christ; *Apart* tells us Christ is the vital connection, and the third word is:

Ask!

"Ask whatever you will, and it shall be done for you." (John 15:7)

If we maintain the vital connection, then we shall have power! This is not a promise that all of our prayers will be answered, "Yes." But it is a promise that even when the answer is no, we shall be given strength sufficient for whatever the need. It is Christ's promise that we shall be given the capacity to deal with life.

As life comes, with all of its changes and choices, we have a tendency to commit several errors. We try to cope in our own strength. (Apart from Christ we can do nothing!) We become preoccupied with our problems, obsessed with them, and nursing and cherishing them without seeking any kind of solution. Erma Bombeck wrote a book entitled, *Aunt Erma's Cope Book* with the sub-title, "How To Get From Monday to Friday — in Twelve Days." It is obviously a take off on all of the self-help books popular today. In a postscript, she concludes with this bit of wisdom from her mother:

> *In her infinite wisdom, my mother offered me yet another observation after my months of self-examination, devotion to improvement, and quest for happiness. She said, "I'll be glad when you hit menopause. It'll take your mind off your problems.*[8]

Sometimes we need to quit nursing our problems and brooding about them — and do something about them!

Another error we make is that we think our faith has nothing to do with life's real problems. We forget that vital religion is connected to life. E. Stanley Jones, the great Methodist Christian, said that we should, "Prepare to preach with one eye on the Bible and the other on the newspaper."[9]

Any preaching, any practice of faith that is meaningful, will be attached to reality, to the real issues of life. We need some faith like the old hymn expressed:

Oh, for a faith that will not shrink,
Though pressed by every foe
That will not stumble on the brink
Of any earthly woe;
A faith that shines forth bright and clear
When troubles rage about;
A faith that in the darkest time,
Will know no doubt.[10]

— William Bathurst

Our faith is always connected to life, and when it is connected to Christ, we have the power to see it through. He promised us "Grace sufficient for our needs." One of the most powerful expressions of this kind of faith was scrawled on the walls of a basement in a German home. The writing was next to a Star of David. It is easy to imagine a family huddled in the damp, dark basement of their home, in fear of their lives because of the Nazi stance against Jews; and there in that darkness, faith was alive when someone wrote:

I believe in the sun even when it is not shining.
I believe in love even when I do not feel it.
I believe in God even when he is silent.[11]

I can promise you, because He has promised us, that if we abide in him, and if we are never apart from that vital connection we can *ask*. We can ask whatever we will, and he will give us sufficient power to see us through. He is the source of our power. He is the vital connection. Christ is the vine, we are the branches, expected to grow, to bear fruit, and to be productive.

I want to make two observations about our faith.

1. *There is a personal dimension*. Ours should be a growing, productive faith that enriches our lives and the lives of those who touch us. A soldier, commenting on the impact of his commanding officer said, "He looked at us and we looked at him; and then we determined to be what he believed us to be."[12]

Something akin to that should be taking place in your spiritual pilgrimage and mine. We should be always looking at Christ. More and more, we should become what he wants us to be, what he believes us to be.

2. *All that we do is for the glory of God*. All that we do and say in our work and in our service should turn the eyes of men and women, not to you, not to me, but to Christ. More and more, they should see more and more of Jesus Christ in our life. John Oxenham said it this way:

> *Is your place a small place?*
> *Tend it with care!*
> *He set you there.*
> *Is your place a large place?*
> *Guard it with care!*
> *He set you there.*
> *What'er your place, it is*
> *Not yours alone, but His*
> *That set you there.*[13]

We need to remember that He is the vine, the source, and we are merely the branches to bear the fruit — so that others might come to know him whom to know is life eternal.

Notes

[1] *The Speaker's Bible, The Gospel According to St. John*, Volume II, edited by the Reverend Edward Hastings, M.A., (Baker Book House, Grand Rapids, Michigan, 1962), p. 92.

[2] Maxie Dunnam, *Jesus's Claims — Our Promises*, (The Upper Room, Nashville, Tennessee, 1985), p. 61.

[3] Richard J. Foster, *Money, Sex, and Power*, (Harper and Row, San Francisco, 1985), p. 44.

[4] *Ibid*, p. 26.

[5] Bruce Larson, *My Creator, My Friend*, (Word Books, Waco, Texas, 1986), p. 41.

[6] *The Interpreter's Bible*, edited by Nolan Harmon, Volume 8, "Luke — John", (Abingdon-Cokesbury Press, Nashville, TN 1952), p. 716.

[7] *The Gospel According to St. John*, "The Speaker's Bible", p. 94.

[8] Erma Bombeck, *Aunt Erma's Cope Book*, (Fawcett, New York, 1981), p. 180.

[9] David L. McKenna, *Renewing Our Ministry*, (Word Books, Waco, Texas, 1986), p. 144.

[10] Robert Schuller, *The Be (Happy) Attitudes*, (Word Books, Waco, Texas, 1985), p. 207.

[11] *Ibid,* p. 211.

[12] William Barclay, *And Jesus Said*, (Westminster Press, Philadelphia, Pennsylvania, 1970), p. 131.

[13] John Oxenham, 1852-1941, by permission of Desmond Dunkerley.

I Am The Light of the World!

Scripture Reading: John 8:1-14
Text: "I am the light of the world." (John 8:12)

There was an early morning confrontation at the temple. The Pharisees brought a woman taken in adultery and they said to Jesus, "The law of Moses says that we should kill her; what do you recommend?"

It seems a rather simple confrontation, but it was far more subtle and complicated than that. It was really a deliberate attempt at entrapment, and here's why:

If Jesus had said, "Stone her," the Jewish leaders would have immediately reported him to the Roman governor and said, "This Jesus of Nazareth is ursurping your power, for only Rome can proclaim a death sentence."

If Jesus has said, "Let her go," they would have immediately accused him of heresy, or disregarding the sacred laws of their religion.

So Jesus, who had gone that morning to the temple to teach, was confronted with a mob mentality. Those accusing the woman were using her to get at Jesus. He did a very wise thing, he stood steady, he did not answer them. He stooped down and began to scribble in the sand. That pause in the electric atmosphere had its effect on those who stood there in self-righteous anger.

How he reacted that day, and what he said to the Pharisees, has some valuable lessons. First of all:

He Challenged Her Accusers!

As they continued to demand an answer from him, he looked up; and I believe that he slowly, but surely, made eye contact with everyone in the mob as they stood there with rocks in hand, ready to toss them. Then Jesus said, "All right hurl the stones at her until she dies. But only he who never sinned may throw the first.'' (John 8:7 [TLB])

Let the perfect ones among you begin the rock throwing. It is one of the most dramatic moments in the life of our Lord. It is a moment that focuses today on your life and mine. How often we accuse, how often we point the finger, and many times we do so to keep others from looking too closely at our own sins. Someone has said that we are often secretly drawn to the sins that we openly decry. Isn't it true that we are more prone to accuse than we are to forgive? Isn't it true that we are quick to believe the worst, and slow to praise the best? When George Whitfield observed a condemned man, a criminal, on the way to the gallows, he uttered his famous sentence, ''There, but for the grace of God, go I.''

It is the first responsibility of the Christian to determine if an accusation is true, and if it is, to seek to understand why the person has fallen. In our understanding there may exist not only the possibility of forgiveness, but of restoration. In any case, before pointing the finger of accusation, or uttering condemning words of judgment, look well into your own heart for sins. Perhaps the very sin you are condemning lurks there as well.

Arnold Toynbee provides a good insight into this as he writes about the city of Los Angeles:

The city is so extensive when measured by the standard of mobility even of the driver of an automobile that the pedestrian visitor is prone to forget that, on the map of the continent as seen by a traveller in an aeroplane, this garden-city which, on the ground, seems boundless, is merely a tiny patch of verdure marooned in the midst of a vast desert. Moreover, the green is so perpetual that the spectator is also prone to forget that it is kept in existence only by a likewise perpetual tour de force. Though on every lawn he sees the sprinklers twisting and turning all day long, he soon comes to take the lawns for granted, as if they had been natural products of a non-existent rainfall. So it gives him a shock when on some vacant lot — kept vacant, perhaps, by a speculator in the hope of rising prices — he sees a savage desert sage-brush bristling up out of a parched and dusty ground. He then realizes that, under the artificial green lawns, the same savage Nature that has here broken its way to the surface is all the time eagerly waiting for an opportunity thus to come into its own again.[1]

As they stood in that mob, fists filled with rocks ready to be tossed, they were challenged by the piercing assertion of Jesus, "If you are without sin throw the first rock."

Is there anyone who could toss a rock? If we are honest before God, we would acknowledge that there are secrets lurking just beneath the surface of our lives which would not look good in the light of day. There are thoughts that cause us shame. There are plans that do not make us proud. There are sins of today and long ago that cause us shame. Many of us are like the character in T. S. Eliot's *Family Reunion*, "We only ask to be reassured about the noises in the cellar." Friends, the noises in the cellar have to be faced, reassurance is not enough.

Mr. Jones hobbled into the pastor's study one day. He leaned the two canes, with which he had walked for twenty-five years, against the desk. Those canes were the result of wounds from World War II. The war had left its mark upon him, and he had come home disabled after serving his country. It was this disabling, crippling wound that made the community tolerate him. He was bad-tempered and irascible. People thought he was still suffering, and so they tolerated his ill-tempered ways the best they could. But, on this day, he had come to the pastor's study to deal with another wound. He confessed that day that he had not been wounded in battle. His crippled condition was the result of a veneral disease. He had been living a lie all those years, and every person whose life had touched his life had been scarred, torn, and bruised by this lie. In the hush of the study, from a torn and agonizing heart, came a question, "Can God forgive me?"[2]

Of course he can! Of course he will. But, we have to acknowledge that the noises in the cellar exist. In T. S. Eliot's play "The Cocktail Party," Edward the despairing husband, is groping in the darkness of his own soul. He cannot love his wife, he cannot rise above his own condemning attitude toward himself. He describs the abyss that is his despair in these words:

There was a door
And I could not open it. I could not touch the handle,
Why could I not walk out of my prison?

It was only yesterday
That damnation took place. And now I must live with it
Day by day, hour by hour, forever and ever.[3]

We do not have to live with our sins forever and ever — we must face them. "The question that belongs to the ages," said J. S. Whale, "is how can I get rid of my sins?"[4] No, we do not have to live with them forever, but we must face them and acknowledge them. That's the first step in getting rid of them.

Jesus challenged the sinner's accusers that day in the early light of morning, and not a rock was thrown. They slipped away pondering the question that belongs to the ages, "How can I get rid of my sins?"

Jesus not only challenged her critics, but note with me also that:

He Had Compassion on the Woman!

As the crowd slipped away, Jesus was left standing with the woman. He said to her, "Where are your accusers? Didn't even one of them condemn you?" (John 8:10 [TLB]) She answered that no one had condemned her and he replied, "Neither do I. Go and sin no more." (John 8:11[TLB])

Can you imagine what those words must have done for that

woman for the rest of her life? In any temptation she could draw strength from his charge, "Go and sin no more."

Of course no one accused her. How could they? The weight of their sins caused them to leave their rocks in the street and slip away. Jesus had compassion on the woman and forgave her sins. She was penitent in her attitude, and she walked away that day forgiven. He had cared for her and had forgiven her. Forgiveness cannot erase the past, but it can heal the wounds of the past.

In the early morning hours at Bellevue Hospital in New York, a man was admitted with a slashed throat. The nurse who tended him had seen his kind from the Bowery before, and would doubtlessly see the likes of him again. He lingered for three days, unable to eat, but asking for water. After he had been dead for several days, a friend came by looking for him. The friend was sent to the city morgue, and there among dozens of others who were unidentified, the friend found Stephen Foster. He was dead at age 38. They found a scrap of paper in his belongings on which was written, "Dear hearts and gentle people." Isn't it tragic that a man who had made his generation sing, and who still makes America sing with songs like "O Susannah," "My Old Kentucky Home," and "Beautiful Dreamer," died uncared for, unknown, and apparently unmissed.[5] I can tell you that sin can do that to you and to me. We need someone to care, to have compassion, to forgive.

Recently I came across these lines from an old poem:

> *And many a man with life out of tune,*
> *And battered and scarred with sin,*
> *Is auctioned cheap to the thoughtless crowd*
> *Much like the old violin.*[6]

Christ said all that was needed to be said that day. He said, "Go and sin no more." The accused woman moved on with compassion, not condemnation — with hope, not despair.

I am more and more convinced that forgiveness is one of

the keys to life and relationships. You cannot live and love in the close proximity of family without forgiveness. You have to give it, and we all need it. Charles Swindoll, in one of his recent books, tells the story of a woman who forgave her husband. It was necessary for her to forgive lest, she journey through life bitter, angry and resentful. Her husband had left her, but one morning she drove to his office and told him that she forgave him. "I told him that the Lord had given me a peace in my life and that I held nothing, absolutely nothing, against him any longer." Many months later, the man came home to her. [7]

Sometimes it does not work out that way, but forgiveness is often the beginning of healing in a relationship. It is not easy to forgive. Forgiveness is not cheap. We always pay for our sins, and pay dearly. Alec Vidler tells a striking story in his book *Christian Belief:*

A tradesman in a certain town found that one of his trusted men had been systematically stealing from his warehouse for years. Some people would have been soft and let him off — other people would have been hardboiled and would have cast the culprit adrift. But this man's employer . . . let him be tried and sentenced and sent to prison. But when he came out of prison his employer was there to greet him with the words, "Your place is open for you. Come back. We will start afresh." And when the man reached home he found that his wages had been paid in full to his wife all the time he had been in prison. He was punished but he was forgiven . . . The forgiveness of God is like that. [8]

I have always loved the story about Abraham Lincoln's pardon of a young soldier. In his first encounter with combat the young soldier had turned and run. For his capitulation he had been sentenced to death. In pardoning the young soldier Lincoln wrote, "I have observed that it does not do a boy much good to shoot him." [9]

We all need to be forgiven. We all need to be more

forgiving. This touching story reminds us of both realities. Jesus challenged the woman's accusers, he had compassion on her, and thirdly:

He Told Her Who He Was!

He said, "I am the light of the world." It is my belief that while the historic roots of this statement lie in the Feast of Tabernacles, its immediate context is with the woman whose life was spared. Her circumstances were dark, but Jesus gave light and hope. Some scholars debate whether or not this story of the street confrontation is really a part of the original manuscripts. While the debate goes on, the reality is that this story has the ring of truth about it. It certainly reflects what we know of the mind, the heart, and the manner of Jesus Christ.

"I am the light of the world," he said. As a part of the Feast of Tabernacles, in the center of the court of the women in the Temple, four great candelabra were lit. A great blaze of light was sent throughout the city of Jerusalem, so that every courtyard in the city was lit up with their brilliance. They burned all night long and the darkness of the city was dispelled.

There is darkness in every life, and we need the light that Christ can give us. What is the function of light? Have you ever thought about it in depth? Light has two functions which seem applicable to life.

1. *Light dispels darkness*. You are sitting in your den and there is a sudden thundershower, and as the rain pelts on the roof, the lights go out. You are suddenly in the dark, and the first thing you think is — where did I last see that flashlight? Or, where are those candles? Once one candle is lit, the darkness is dispelled, because the focus is on that one single light. There may be shadows here and there, but darkness no longer dominates. There needs to be a light shining in the darkness of your life and mine. That is why Christ came — to bring light into our darkness!

Christ not only said that he was "the light of the world" but that "he who follows me will not walk in darkness." (John 8:12) The darkness of our lives gives way to the forgiving love and light of Christ. When we forgive another, and when we are forgiven by Christ, his light shines in our darkness. As a boy C. S. Lewis was badly scarred and hurt by a bully of a man who taught in an English School Lewis attended. The teacher was a cruel individual who made life a living torment for his pupils. Years later, C. S. Lewis acknowledged that he could not forgive the teacher, and that his lack of capacity to forgive troubled him. But just a few months before he died, Lewis was able to forgive this teacher and wrote these words to a friend in America:

Dear Mary,
*   Do you know, only a few weeks ago I realized suddenly that I had forgiven the cruel schoolmaster who so darkened my childhood. I'd been trying to do it for years; and like you, each time I thought I'd done it, I found, after a week or so it all had to be attempted over again. But this time I feel sure it is the real thing."*[10]

You see light had come for Lewis, where there was once darkness there was now light.

Some years ago, I received an urgent telephone call from a seminary classmate. I could tell he was under stress, his voice broke as we talked. He said, "There is a letter in the mail to you, read it, and let me hear from you. I need to hear from you, don't turn me down."

I asked if we could talk about it over the phone and he said he could not talk about it. He urged me, "Please read my letter and let me hear from you." I promised him I would do so.

I received the letter, and in it my former classmate had poured out his heart. It was a shocking letter in some ways. He begged my forgiveness for all the ways he had hurt me. He asked forgiveness for the jealousy he felt toward me, and for all of the backbiting, underhanded things he had done to harm me and my ministry. To say the least, I was stunned. I was completely and totally unaware of any of what he was telling me. I was not aware of any hurt he had caused me. The final sentence of his letter will never leave my memory. "I need your forgiveness. I can no longer live with myself for the harm I feel I have caused you."

He had caused me no harm, he had only injured himself. I immediately called him and told him that all was well, and that I forgave him. I cannot describe the obvious joy my old friend expressed to me when I said to him, "I forgive you." It was light into his darkness. Christ offers light to you and to me. He is the light of the world.

Light not only dispels darkness, it:

2. *Reveals the way.* As the *Living Bible* paraphrases it, "If you follow me, you won't be stumbling through the darkness, for living light will flood your path." (John 8:12)

When the lights go out at your house you don't have to stumble around in the darkness, stub your toes, bang your shins, and walk into doors that are half open. You find a flashlight or candle, and the light points out the way you should walk, a way unhindered, unhampered by obstructions. Because with light to help you find the way, you can avoid those obstacles that would be in your path. There is no need for us to stumble and fall, if we follow the light Christ provides.

Light is a positive force. Many people make religion a negative thing. It is positive, don't ever forget that. Light casts out darkness, and that is positive.

Dwight Moody said, "People have just enough religion to make themselves miserable; they cannot be happy at a wild party and they are uncomfortable at a prayer meeting."[11]

That is true. Many people have just enough religion to make themselves, and everybody around them, miserable. Many people who say they love Christ and walk in his way have a negative witness. I know of many Christians who seem to have a hammer in their hands, going about looking for nails to hit.

Nothing could be a grosser misrepresentation of what Christ wants. What he wants is positive; it is light casting out the darkness.

The whole concept of light is awesome; it dispels darkness, it shows the way. Nothing is hidden. But, it is of no use whatever if *we do not walk in the light*. If we do not take Christ at his word and walk in his light — then it is as if he never came. Spiritually, we are still stumbling and bumbling around in the dark. We often talk more faith than we live.

One of the great sins of the ministry is to preach more faith than we live. There is an ancient prayer that says:

> *From the cowardice that shrinks from new truth,*
> *From the laziness that is content with half-truth,*
> *From the arrogance that thinks it knows all truth,*
> *O God of truth, deliver us.*[12]

It is true that cowardice, laziness, arrogance keep us from responding fully to the best of our abiility; and we play all kinds of games to keep from dealing with what is reality.

I read a story recently that has nagged at me for days. A truck driver was making his way across town, studiously following the prescribed route for trucks. But there was something different about this driver. Every time he came to a stop sign or traffic light, he would jump out of his truck with a baseball bat in his hands and repeatedly beat the side of the truck. He did this again and again. A curious driver in the car behind the truck observed this strange behavior, and when the truck pulled into a restaurant parking lot it was more than he could stand. He pulled in behind the truck, got out of his car and asked the truck driver, "Why do you beat your truck with a bat every time you stop?"

The truck driver was patient and happy to answer. He said, "Well, it is like this. I have a two-ton truck and four tons of canaries, and I have to keep two tons in the air all the time."[13]

Isn't that a parable of so many of our lives? We are overloaded with all kinds of excess baggage, and instead of facing the reality, we are just trying to re-arrange the load. In the musical, "Big River," Huck Finn sings what I feel to be the most moving song in the play, "I have lived in the darkness for so long, I am waiting for the light to shine." During the dramatic moment of confrontation in the life of Jesus, he met the test. He challenged the woman's accusers, and they dropped their stones and slipped away. He had compassion on the woman, he forgave her. He told her who he was, "I am the light of the world." But notice how the Pharisees replied to Jesus, "You are boasting and lying." (John 8:13 [TLB])

They rejected the light that was offered. We still have that choice. We can continue to muddle through the dark, or can we respond to the light of Christ. I am sure you remember from history lessons the name, "Sutter's Hill, California." That is where James w. Marshall discovered gold in Sutter's Creek in 1848. That discovery started the great California Gold Rush of 1849. People came from all over this country and beyond, driven by the desire for gold. In 1880, near a place called Auburn, California, in an abandoned mine shaft, the body of a gold miner was found. It was James Marshall, the same man who had discovered the gold that started the Rush of 1849. Here, thirty-one years later, the man who had set into motion events that led to fortunes for many, died penniless because he had never taken the time to stake his own claim.[14]

It is a parable of life for many today. In a society, in a culture, molded, shaped, and influenced by Christian truth, the values Christ stood for and taught seem so commonplace that many walk in darkness — simply because they never stake a claim. Many never make the choice to come out of the darkness and walk in the light.

In a short story by Hermann Hesse, these searching, sobering, arresting words appear:

Life passes like a flash of lightening,
Whose blaze barely lasts long enough to see.

While the earth and the sky stand still forever,
How swiftly changing time flies across man's face.
O you who sit over your full cup and do not drink,
Tell me, for whom are you still waiting?[15]

Notes

[1] Sir Arnold Toynbee, *An Historian's Approach to Religion*, (Oxford Press, New York, 1956), p. 24.

[2] William H. Hinson, *Solid Living In A Shattered World*, (Abingdon Press, Nashville, 1985), p. 56.

[3] From *The Cocktail Party*, copyright 1950 by T. S. Eliot; renewed 1978 by Esme Valerie Eliot. Reprinted by permission of Harcourt Brace Jovanovich, Inc.

[4] Robert E. Luccock, "Our Exceeding Need and God's Exceeding Love," from *The Power of His Name,* (Harper and Brothers Publishers, New York, New York, 1960), p. 65.

[5] Charles R. Swindoll, *Come Before Winter*, (Multnomah Press, Portland, Oregon, 1985), p. 36.

[6] *Ibid*, p. 37

[7] Charles R. Swindoll, *Living On The Ragged Edge*, (Word Books, Waco, Texas, 1985), p. 318.

[8] Alex Vidler, *Christian Belief*, (Charles Scribner's Sons, 1950) p. 96.

[9] Cliff C. Jones, *Winning Through Integrity*, (Abingdon Press, Nashville, Tennessee, 1985), p. 64.

[10] Lewis B. Smedes, *Forgive and Forget*, (Harper and Row Publishers, San Francisco, CA, 1984), p. 95.

[11] Robert Schuller, *The Be (Happy) Attitudes*, (Word Books, Waco, Texas, 1985), p. 118.

[12] Cliff C. Jones, *Winning Through Integrity*, p. 35.

[13] Tim Timmons and Stephen Artenburn, *Hooked On Life*, (Oliver Nelson, A Division of Thomas Nelson, Nashville, TN, 1985), p. 28

[14] Zig Ziglar, *Raising Positive Kids In A Negative World*, (Oliver Nelson, A Divison of Thomas Nelson, Nashville, TN 1985), pp. 45-46.

[15] Hermann Hesse, "Klingsor's Last Summer," Copyright by Farrar, Straus and Grioux, Inc., 1970. Reprinted by permission of Farrar, Straus and Grioux, Inc.

I Am Alpha and Omega!

Scripture Reading: Revelation 1:1-8
Text: "I am Alpha and Omega." (Revelation 1:8)

John, the last living disciple, was alone, old, and in exile. He was cut off from home and familiar things. The Roman Emperors had declared that the official policy of the state was to eradicate, remove, or destroy the followers of Christ. To put it mildly, it was a dangerous time to be a Christian. All John could do was to wait and wonder. Being human he had to be alternately worried and afraid, wondering what the days would bring.

I am sure there were times, as John waited and wondered about the future, that scenes from his long and useful life flashed before his mind. He must have reflected on moments of fellowship with our Lord, and the faces of people touched by Christ's ministry along the way. He surely remembered that day of searing pain and death when Christ was crucified. He was the only disciple who was there. All the others had fled the scene — Peter had denied him — Judas, in utter remorse, had taken his own life — but now all John had was prayer and memories.

His days were now filled with anxiety and anticipation. Anxiety for those who were having to suffer, and anticipation that soon his own time would come. Then it happened. The record states that he was "in the spirit on the Lord's Day" (Revelation 1:10), and he heard a voice like a great trumpet sounding, saying, "I am alpha and omega, the first and the last." (Revelation 1:11)

We are dealing with powerful symbols when we look at our text. The most obvious observation is that *alpha* is the first letter of the Greek alphabet, and *omega* is the last. It speaks of a God of completeness, one who is sure, steadfast, whatever the time. He is there at the beginning of things. When life emerges, when the human pilgrimage starts, God is there.

We have little, or no, control over the beginning of our lives. I remember as a boy having a conversation with my father's oldest brother, my Uncle Burton. My father was the youngest of ten children. My Uncle Burton waxed very eloquently that day when he said, "Son, I remember when your daddy was a boy just like you. I remember when he started to school, when he went off to serve in World War I, when he came home from France, and he and your mother were married. Then, looking at me he said, "I knew your mama and daddy long before you were even a gleam in their eyes!"

We had little to do with our beginnings, with the accident or the circumstances of our birth. It was beyond our cognition or our control, but God knew about it and was there, for he is *alpha*. So give thanks today for the blessings and bounty of your birth.

He is there, also, at the end of things. Omega is the last letter of the Greek alphabet, and it speaks of completion. We have little, or no, control over the ending of life, either. The doctors tell us that we can enhance the quality of our living and prolong our days a bit by eating right, exercising consistently, jogging a bit, living moderately, abstaining from drinking and smoking — but even with all of that our time will come. The Psalmist, speaking of our earthly journey, said:

In the morning they are like grass which grows up: in the morning it flourishes and grows up; in the evening it is cut down and withers. (Psalm 90:5-6)

We finish our years like a sigh. (Psalm 90:9)

So teach us to number our days, that we may gain a heart of wisdom. (Psalm 90:12)

We are literally here today and gone tomorrow. Dennis Barnhart was the chief executive of Eagle Computer, Incorporated, a company that started small, grew rapidly, and finally went public. He was forty-four years old when the stock went public and he became a multi-millionaire overnight. Then one afternoon, a few blocks from his office, he drove his red Farrari through twenty feet of guard rail into a ravine and died. The afternoon of the accident his 592,000 shares were worth more than nine million dollars.[1]

We have little or no control over our ending, but God does, for he is *alpha* and *omega*. He is there undergirding it all. The text gives a strong hint at the staying power of Christ, for John describes him as the one, who is, who was, and who is to come. The message is clear: whether undergoing persecution, or exiled on the Island of Patmos, or confronted with the challenges of life in 20th century America, Christ is the one certainty we can hold on to in this world. Some unknown pilgrim with a poetic bent put pen to paper one day and gave birth to these lines:

> *My times are in thy hand:*
> *I'll always trust in thee,*
> *And, after death, at thy right hand,*
> *I shall forever be.*

He is always with us, whatever the circumstances, whether beginning or ending. When Abe Lincoln was ready to depart from Springfield, Illinois on the journey to Washington to assume the office of the Presidency, friends gathered to tell him goodbye. They knew the burdens facing him and wanted to give him a supportive sendoff. Among those who visited that day was an elderly Quaker woman. When all the others began to leave, she lingered behind. Then she took Mr. Lincoln by the hand and whispered in his ear, "Friend Abraham, God will surely go with thee. Even in thy mansion with all its room, His footsteps will be beside thine."

Years later, with war raging — dissension among his closest associates — plots of assassination all around him — those whispered words sustained Abraham Lincoln. After he was cruelly assassinated, they found in his desk a paper, in his handwriting, with these words, "God will surely go with thee."[2]

In studying this text I have seen something new. It is the fact that you have, I have, no control over the beginning of things in life, or the end of things in life. The reality that all of us are here means that we have moved beyond *alpha* and have not yet reached *omega*. We are struggling with life in the "in between times," between already and not yet. What does Christ offer us now? I believe he offers us three things as we struggle and strive between *alpha*, when things began for us, and *omega*, when things will end.

First of all,

He Loves Us!

Our text says it plainly, "To him who loved us." (Revelation 1:5)

The Bible defines God as love. In fact, it wants you to know, above all else, that the one central impulse at the heart of God is love. He is always, in every way, everywhere loving us, wooing us, trying to win us to himself. When life tumbles in on us, one of the first things we want to know is how we stand with God. A man, aged forty-five, came to see me some months ago. He told me that he had had a terminal diagnosis of cancer. His doctor had told him that day that he had, at the outside, about two months to live. He actually lived five weeks. But he said to me, "Does that mean that God does not love me anymore?" No, it didn't mean that at all. About a week before he died, he discovered it was true; he knew that God still loved him.

A mother said to me, in the context of her daughter having been killed in a wreck, "Has God turned his back on us as a family?"

In the book, *How Green Was My Valley*, by Richard Llewellyn, Gwilymn Morgan is crushed to death in a collapsing mine shaft. In her grief, Mrs. Morgan hurls the verdict of "guilty" into the face of God, as she says, "God could have had him a hundred ways . . . but He had to have him like that.

A beetle under the foot . . . if I set foot in Chapel again, it will be in my box, and knowing nothing of it.''³

The hurts we experience, the disappointments that burden us, the dreams that vanish, the child that rebels, the spouse that is unfaithful, the illness that debilitates, the friend that betrays — none of it, I promise you, none of it ever separates us from God's capacity to love us. His love is always operative and available, through good times, through bad times. That truth can make a difference in your life.

The older I get, the more I realize how important it is for us to be loved. It is very important for us to love our children. If you do nothing else for your child but consistently love him or her, that is the most important thing you can do. Many lives never develop, never really get under way because of the feeling of being unwanted and unloved. Many problems in life grow out of a lack of self-esteem — within people who have not been adequately loved.

Let me tell you about such a person. This young man had a very strong willed, domineering mother. She had been married three times. Her second husband left her because she regularly beat him up. The father of the young man I am telling you about was her third husband, who died of a heart attack shortly before his boy was born. The boy's mother had to work long hours as he was growing up. He received very little affection from her, and almost no discipline. He experienced very little love, and so he gave little love. He became a loner. Despite a high IQ, he did poorly academically and never graduated from high school. He joined the marines, but was not accepted there either; He resisted authority and was finally given an undesirable discharge.

So, cast adrift in his early twenties, scrawny, already getting bald, he went to live in another country. While there, he married a girl who had been an illegitimate child and brought her back to this country with him. In a short time she developed a contempt for him, and made demands on him that he could not meet. She dominated him just as his mother had done.

She forced him to leave, but he came back again and begged her to take him in. She belittled him, called him a failure, and once made fun of his sexual impotency before a friend.

A private nightmare engulfed him; no one wanted him, it was the story of his life. He was a lonely, unloved, desperate man. One day he got up, and there was a strange calmness about him. He went to the garage, took down a rifle he had been hiding there; he carried it to work with him, and shortly after noon on November 22, 1963, he sent two shells crashing into the head of President John Fitzgerald Kennedy.[4]

Every time I read the story of Lee Harvey Oswald's life, I remember how important it is for us to love. If no one else in this world loves you, or even thinks about you, God does, and don't you forget it! If you will let the reality of his love grip you, it can, and it will, make a difference. There are many people today who feel unloved. Remember, God loves you. He sent Christ to show it, to reveal it fully, to assure us of his love forever.

It is our task to let the love of God through Christ shine through our lives, so that others can feel it and experience it and know it. We often think of the Christian faith in some heroic dimension — show me a mountain to climb, a river to cross, or some act of martyrdom and great courage that I must muster. None of that is going to happen to the vast majority of us. We are charged with the responsibility of being a witness for Christ and his love every day, with everyone we meet.

I love the story of the man who walked into a restaurant, one of those garden variety greasy spoon restaurants, where there is a warm smile, and good food reasonably priced. The man behind the counter said, "O.K. Mac, what's your pleasure?" The answer quickly came, "Two fried eggs and a few kind words." Soon the waiter returned, slapped the eggs down on the table, and started to walk off when the customer said to him, "Hey, Friend, you forgot the few kind words." The waiter replied, "Oh yeah . . . Don't eat dem eggs."[5]

A few kind words can often show the love of God in us — and the love of Christ working through us. Is that too much to ask in the "between times" between *alpha* and *omega*? We should rejoice in the reality that God loves us, and show that love to others.

Longfellow has written:

> *Nor father or mother has loved you as God has, for it was that you might be happy when He gave His only Son. When He bowed His head in the death hour, love solemnized its triumph; the sacrifice there was complete.*[6]

Somewhere, on the walls of an insane asylum, someone discovered these very sane words of joy:

> *Could we with ink the oceans fill*
> *And were the skies of parchment made*
> *And every stalk on earth a quill*
> *And every man a scribe by trade.*
>
> *To write the love of God above*
> *Would drain the oceans dry,*
> *Nor could that scroll contain the whole*
> *Though stretched from sky to sky.*[7]

Those who live and struggle between "already" and "not yet" need to remember that he loves us!

There is hope — the God of completeness, who in Christ is both *alpha* and *omega*, not only loves us, but he has:

Loosed Us From Our Sins!

Our text puts it this way, "sets us free from our sins." (Revelation 1:5) Another translation captures it this way, "washed us from our sins in His own blood." He not only set us free, it was a costly release.

Sin has social, corporate, community complications, but

it is always rooted in a personal condition. We need to remember the incisive observation of Saint Augustine who said, "Never fight evil as if it were something that arose totally outside of yourself." Sin is always rooted in self.

I grew up in rural South Carolina and the traditions of family and church were closely woven together. The farm was a fairly self-contained unit. My playmates — swimming, fishing, hunting companions — were black. Because of this, I was exposed to a great deal of black preaching. Most of the black ministers in our neighborhood knew my father. I frequently attended some of their services of worship. There is something deeply moving about the effective preaching of our black brothers of the cloth. They are steeped in the Bible. Many of those I knew as a boy taught themselves to read by reading the Bible. They imployed vivid imagery, and held an exalted view of God.

They were at their best in describing both the conditions and the consequences of sin. They rooted sin in individual responsibility. James Weldon Johnson in "God's Trombones" captures both the content and the flavor of black preaching. Let me share a bit of this with you, as the black preacher deals with the theme of the after-life, when time shall be no more:

> *Oh-O-Oh, sinner,*
> *Where will you stand*
> *In that great day when God's a-going*
> *to rain down fire?*
> *Oh, you gambling man — where will you stand?*
> *Your whore-mongering man — where will you stand?*
> *Liars and backsliders — where will you stand,*
> *In that great day when God's a-going*
> *to rain down fire?*[8]

I can tell you where we will stand, we will stand in the hands of a loving God who in Christ has loosed us from our sins. Fanny Crosby picked that up in one of her great hymns:

Touched by a loving heart,
Awakened by kindness,
Chords that were broken
Will vibrate once more.

In the "in-between time," where we struggle between *alpha* and *omega*, the God of completion has provided for you and for me. He loves us, he has loosed us from our sins, and:

He Lets Us Love Him!

The New Testament defines the kingdom of God, not in territorial terms, but in relational terms. Our text says it this way, Christ "made us kings and priests to his God and Father." (Revelation 1:6) *The Living Bible* captures it in these words, he "gathered us into his kingdom."

He not only loves us, he lets us love him. We can relate to him in a personal way. Elton Trueblood has written that for God to matter to us, he must be met, not just discussed and argued about, but met — personally known.

The longer I live, the more convinced I am that we cannot make it through this world on our own strength. The accumulation of unanswered questions, the riddles of life that the human mind cannot grasp, the tragedies we observed that tear the soul and challenge our faith — all of it adds up to a sense of inadequacy in the face of life. We all need, not a creed, not a set of rules, but a relationship — and that is what Christ offers to us. Somewhere, William Barclay records a conversation he had with a psychiatrist. A friend was undergoing therapy and Dr. Barclay said, "I suppose that when he comes out of this hospital he will be quite cured, repressions, inhibitions, complexes gone, a new man."

The psychiatrist replied, "We can only strip a man naked until we see him as he is: and if when we have done that, he is bad stuff, we can't do a thing about it. That's where you come in."[9]

We are all "bad stuff" when we are stripped naked before God, and Christ is the greatest healer of them all. He heals us by letting us love him back, by gathering us into his kingdom, a kingdom which the New Testament defines as relationships.

"I am alpha and omega," He said. He is the God who completes. He is with us at the first, and he is with us at the last. I read a play some time back entitled, "The Terrible Meek," and in the play the centurion who stood at the foot of the Cross turned, when Christ was dead, and said to Mary, "I tell you, woman, that this dead Son of yours — disfigured, shamed, spat upon, has built this day a kingdom that can never die."[10] Has he? Are you a part of his kingdom? Is your life made different by the knowledge that he loves you, that he has loosed you from your sins, and because you have accepted the offer of love to relate to him? I remember an American success story, far too typical for comfort. This man made himself famous in the catering business. He built a chain of restaurants across this country. And as he lay dying, his relatives gathered about his bed. Someone bent over to hear his final words, and his last whisper was, "Slice the ham thin."[11]

Facing his destiny, is that all — is that *all* he could say? We live in the time between *alpha* and *omega*. But, when *omega* comes, as it will for each one of us, what will he find us doing?

Maxie Dunnam in his chapter on this text ends by asking a series of questions. Questions that are worth remembering. When he comes:

Will he find us
witnessing to his saving grace to our
neighbors, friends, and colleagues?

Will he find us
actively engaged in protesting all that
which profanes and limits life?

Will he find us
making peace in every way possible?

Will he find us
doing that which he said would be the criteria
By which we would be judged "sheep" or "goats"
that is
Feeding the hungry,
Clothing the naked,
Caring for the prisoners,
Visiting the sick?[12]

What will he find us doing when he comes?

I read about a law firm in Baltimore that was moving to new offices. You know how law firms send out those formal announcements. Someone got the announcement from the law firm on the same day he heard that a friend had died. He decided to respond to both realities by sending flowers. Unfortunately, the florist got the cards mixed up. The bouquet that arrived at the law firm had a card that read, "Deepest Sympathy." And if you think that is bad, the card that arrived at the funeral home for the family of the deceased friend read, "Congratulations on your new location."[13]

We are all going to have a new location one day. Trust in Christ for your destination.

A poor woman was ordering a tombstone for her deceased husband. She did not want anything elaborate, so she told the stone cutter to make it simple, and left these instructions, "Just carve his name and put on there, 'to my husband' in a suitable place." To her dismay, when she viewed the final product at the gravesite it read, "To my husband in a suitable place."[13]

We are living in "between-times" now, between *alpha* and *omega*, preparing to move to a new location. My prayer is that it will be a suitable place.

Longfellow would have been remembered if these lines were all he ever wrote:

Lives of great men all remind us
We can make our lives sublime,

And, departing, leave behind us
  Footprints on the sands of time.

What kind of tracks are you making today? We need to make these days count for Jesus Christ.

Notes

[1] Los Angeles Times, June 10, 1983.

[2] Frank H. Seilhamer, *Adventure In Faith*, (New World Press, York, Pennsylvania, 1982), p. 42.

[3] John N. Gladstone, *The Valley of the Verdict*, (Abingdon Press, Nashville and New York, 1960), p. 74.

[4] James Dobson, *Hide or Seek*, (Fleming H. Revell, Old Tappan, New Jersey, 1974), pp. 9-10.

[5] William Sloane Coffin, Living The Truth In A World Of Illusions, (Harper and Row Publishers, San Francisco, 1985), p. 41.

[6] Ted W. Engstrom, *The Fine Art Of Friendship*, (Thomas Nelson Publishers, Nashville, 1985), p. 121.

[7] *Ibid*, p. 121.

[8] James Weldon Johnson, *God's Trombones*, Copyright 1927, Viking Press, Inc., Copyright renewed 1955 by Grace Nail Johnson. Any reprint permission only of Viking Penquin, Inc.

[9] Gladstone, *The Valley Of The Verdict*, p. 118.

[10] By Ian MacPherson, ed. *More Sermons I Should Like To Have Preached*, (Fleming H. Revell Company, Westwood, New Jersey, 1977) p. 51.

[11] Ibid, p. 144.

[12] Maxie Dunnam, *Jesus' Claims — Our Promises*, (The Upper Room, Nashville, Tennessee, 1985), p. 113. Used by permission of the publisher.

[13] Bruce Larson, *My Creator, My Friend*, (Word Books, Waco, Texas, 1986), p. 191.

[14] *Ibid*, p. 192.

I Am A King!

Scripture Reading: John 18:28-40
Text: Pilate replied, "But you are a king then?" "Yes," Jesus said, "I was born for that purpose. And I came to bring truth to the world. All who love the truth are my followers." (John 18:37[TLB])

It was a week that began with the shout of *Hosanna*, and ended with a mob angrily demanding, "Crucify him!" "Crucify him!" It was a week that began with Jesus entering Jerusalem in triumph, and ended with him staggering under the dead weight of a Roman cross as he made his way, under armed guards, to the place of death. How could the mood change so quickly? How could events move to such a tragic end? I can tell you that it happened that way because of the manipulations of the power elite. Religious and political power joined hands out of self interests to put Jesus of Nazareth to death.

As we look into the events of the final evening of the earthly pilgrimage of Jesus — the Last Supper is over; Judas has completed his act of betrayal; Jesus had been arrested in the Garden of Gethsemane; Peter had now denied him; and "kangaroo justice" was beginning to unfold — they wanted a verdict of guilty; only the appearance of legality would be maintained, and that would soon be cast aside. Only the Roman Governor, Pilate, had the legal authority to pronounce a death sentence. When Pilate heard the evidence, he concluded that Jesus was innocent. (John 18:38;19:4)

The confrontation began with a question, "Are you king of the Jews?" (John 19:33) It ends when Jesus asserts, "My kingdom is not of this world." (John 18:36) But he asserted that he was a king when he said, "I was born for that purpose. And I came to bring truth to the world. All who love the truth are my followers." (John 18:37 [TLB])

How shall we respond to his claim to be a king? Even as we note that his "kingdom is not of this world" we must acknowledge that:

We Think of Kings in Terms of Power

Not the power of rhetoric, not the power of moral persuasion, but real power, the kind of power the world notices. The power of military might, the power of enormous financial strength, the power to move and shake things if the need should arise.

I have seen or met every President since Dwight Eisenhower. I can tell you that one of the impressions you get when you meet a President is that of power. When he arrives bands play, soldiers snap to attention and fire a twenty-one gun salute. At a word from the President planes fly, soldiers march, and ships sail. It all speaks of power. With a stroke of his pen a resolution from Congress becomes a law to be obeyed. It speaks of power.

On two occasions Sara and I have been present when the Queen of England and other members of the royal family arrived. There was pomp and circumstance to be sure, much of it rooted in heritage and history, but behind it all was the reality of power. When Prince Charles came to Atlanta, we were invited to a reception for him, and met and chatted with the future King of England. I can tell you that as a person he was utterly charming, but security aides hovered near, and there was about this royal visitor the aura of power.

We always associate earthly rulers with presidents, sultans, kings, queens, with power. They say "go" and people go. They say "come" and people come. I am sure, with human nature being what it is, this "power" can be corrupting if they are not careful. Harry S Truman alluded to this on one occasion when he said that the President was in trouble if he concluded that "Hail to the Chief" was being played for him, rather than for the office of the President of the United States. If you will read the New Testament and note the teachings of Jesus, you will see that he talked a great deal about money and about power. The demon in money is greed. The demon in power is pride. Both can so dominate a life that nothing else matters. Both can absorb the human spirit. Make no mistake about it, we think of kings, presidents, Prime ministers, in terms of power. And — so did those who plotted, planned, and executed the death of Jesus of Nazareth. They saw him as a threat to their power.

As the story of their crime against the fairest this world has ever known unfolds, we see power politics at its worst. We see vested interests joining ranks to protect, to defend their positions of privilege and power. Their objective was to remove Jesus of Nazareth as a threat; their means — anything that would achieve his removal. Just look at what they did to reach their objective:

. . . They instigated an illegal trial, the religious leaders utterly disregarding their own laws.

. . . They bribed a trusted member of the disciple band and left him, in his remorse and despair, to take his own life. I am sure that when they heard he was dead they were relieved, because no court of inquiry could call him to testify against them.

. . . They shifted the accusations against Jesus to suit the forum. Before the Jews and religious authorities, the charge was blasphemy. Before Pilate, it was insurrection, treasonous activity directed at the overthrow of the established authority of Rome. The accusation was tailored to fit the bias of the forum they were before. The fact that both accusations were false did not matter.

. . . They intimidated and threatened his followers, pushing Peter to denial with vehement cursing.

. . . The scent of death was in the air and all of his disciples, save one, fled the city.

They had succumbed to the age old threat of power, that "might makes right." To wit, I call to your remembrance Marcos of the Philipines, Duvalier of Haiti, and the government of South Africa. *Might* does not make right. I shall never forget being present when Bishop Tutu said:

> *We just want to be free! Free to embrace our children as they run to us at eventide. Free to live with our families and enjoy the family circle! We just want to be free!*

And God means for us to be free. Power is an elixer that many want to drink. It can be used for good, but it can be used for evil as well. You know the statement, "Power corrupts — absolute power corrupts absolutely." Marcos and Duvalier are now diplomatic obscenities, pariahs, respected by no one, wanted by no country on earth because of their corruption.

We must recognize both the dangers and limits of power. One of the dangers of the ministry is power. There is an enormous power and influence that is given to the pastoral office over a period of years. It is the accumulation of relationships. It is the gratitude of a grateful people that have been faithfully served. It is the power of confidence and confidentiality. It is the power of proclamation. I preach twice every Sunday, and no one interrupts or talks back. I get all kinds of feedback — some praise, some critical. (I loved some of the comments that come to me after the Ash Wednesday service. This was a very moving service in which the congregation members were asked to write on pieces of paper the sins and bad habits that hindered them from being fully committed Christians. They then brought those pieces of paper to the altar, deposited them into an urn, where they were burned. A symbolism, to be sure, of how quickly God forgives us for our sins and wrong doings. One person suggested that we change the name of the church to, "The Church of the Holy Smoke." Another person expressed concerns about being in a church where it took two urns to hold all of the sins.)

Even in the ministry, there is a danger in power. One of the most interesting and incisive comments about power came from Napoleon. He said:

The more I study the world, the more I am convinced of the inability of force to create anything durable. Alexander, Caesar, Charlemagne, and even I myself have founded empires; but upon what did they depend? They depended upon force, but Jesus Christ built His empire upon love, and until this day millions will die for him.[1]

We think of kings in terms of power — the capacity to force their will. Jesus said that he was a king, but what kind of king? He also said,

My Kingdom Will Be Different!

You remember how he said it, "My kingdom is not of this world." (John 18:36)

It was Passover time, the city was crowded with pilgrims from all over the world. They had come to celebrate the crucial moment of their history, when they were delivered by God, when slaves became a people. When Jesus entered the city, they were electrified because they saw him as *King Jesus*. He had fed the masses. He had healed the sick. His miracles were well known. His teachings had about them the ring of truth. The people heard him gladly, for they just knew that he was the one to lead them once again to freedom. But his kingdom was not to be of this world, it was to be of the heart — the way of love which the world still has difficulty comprehending. Harry Kemp captured it in his poem, "The Conquerors."

I saw the Conquerors riding by
 With cruel lips and faces wan:
Musing on kingdoms sacked and burned
 There rode the Mongol Genghis Khan;

And Alexander, like a god,
 Who sought to weld the world in one:
And Caesar with his laurel wreath;
 And like a thing from Hell, the Hun:

And leading like a star the van,
  Heedless of upstretched arm and groan,
Inscrutable Napleon went
  Dreaming of empire, and alone . . .

Then all they perished from the earth.
  As fleeting shadows from a glass,
And, conquering down the centuries,
  Came Christ, the Swordless, on an ass![2]

No armies to seize power. No troops to maintain his power and position. A kingdom based on truth and love, where those who followed would practice love and seek the truth, where needs of neighbor would equal concern for self. A kingdom where cheeks would be turned, where second miles would be walked, where cloaks would be given to cover the nakedness of one who had no cloak, where enemies would be prayed for, not hated, where persecutors would feel the pressure of the Golden Rule, where sharing would be more prevalent than shoving, where hate would give way to love, where caring would overcome indifference, and where truth would be stronger than falsehood.

We shall not see the arrival of that kingdom this side of heaven itself, but I can tell you this, that in the reaching, in the responding, in the risking to bringing it to pass here on earth, we shall be striving toward our highest dream and our deepest satisfaction.

I can tell you that Pilate knew little of the kingdom Christ talked about, and most of us know little of it. Jesus has endured a two thousand year frustration, for we still think in terms of power when he wants us to think of love. So little of what he taught has been received and practiced.

Let me call the roll of what he wants of us in this kingdom of his, in light of what we consistently give him.

He said, that in his kingdom, *humility would be the test of greatness.* We would be servers, not served. James Denney said that, "no man can exalt Christ and himself at the self-same moment.''[3] How little of humility and serving we see in our lives. It is so easy to let self-interest become the focus of our lives. Again, and again the Bible warns us not to think more highly of ourselves than we ought to think. Recently, Sara and I went to Converse College where our daughter Susi was in a play, Christopher Marlow's *Dr. Faustus.* She played Faustus, and we, of course, thought she was great. There is a line in that play about one of the great mythological figures, Icarus, that is worth remembering.

Til swollen with the cunning of a self conceit his waxen wings did mount above his reach and melting, heavens conspired his overthrow. (Dr. Faustus — Act 1)

So conceited was he that he flew too high and destroyed himself. This can happen to you, to me. In Christ's kingdom, humility would be the true test of greatness. A humility that seeks ways to serve, rather than demands to be served.

In his kingdom, he said, that *love would be the best way of them all.* Love that expects nothing in return. Two Lutheran pastors have just written a thought-provoking book called *The Penguin Principles* with the intriguing sub-title "A Survival Manual for Clergy Seeking Maturity in Ministry." The opening chapter of the book is called "The Five Percent Principle," and this is what they say:

Despite the pious things we say, at any given time, less than five percent of any group of people in the church is operating with purely Christian motivation. The other ninety-five percent is asking, "What's in it for me?"[4]

It just may be, that if they are right, this is the reason for the church's lack of power today. The direction is inward rather than reaching out in love. The flow of our energy is focused on self rather than on service. In Christ's kingdom, love is asking the question, "What can I do, in Christ's name for you?" It never asks the question, "What's in it for me?"

In his kingdom humility is the test of greatness, love is the best way of them all, and *fear gives way to faith.* In his kingdom we are not beset with our fears, but living life in response to faith. Isn't it true that in most instances, most of the time, we are trying to live our lives in our own strength? We have a tendency to think of the resources of faith only when something big comes down upon us.

A minister friend of mine tells a delightful story about the reading habits of his grandmother, who lived in their home while he was in high school. She loved to read, and so he would seek out books by her favorite authors and take them to her. He noticed that every time he brought her a book, she would immediately turn to the final chapter and read it. He simply could not understand that, because for him reading the last chapter would spoil the book, so he asked her about it. Without the slightest hesitation she said to him. "If I don't like the way a book ends, I don't see any sense wasting my time reading it."[5]

There is a lesson here worth remembering. Friends, our faith assures us that the outcome of events is in God's hands, and that it is positive and redemptive. This ought to enable us to live without so much fear.

In his kingdom, a kingdom not of this world, humilty, not arrogance will be prevalent; love, not hate, will be at the forefront; faith will be more obvious than fear, and *giving will be more evident than getting.* There is so much greed operative in our world and in our lives. Some of us need to stop and ask, "How much is enough?" Then, having reflected on that question, we should consider what we can give back to the God who has blessed us so abundantly. How seldom we pause to give thanks for the bounty we have received. How often do you say a prayer of Thanksgiving to God? Isn't it true that much of our praying is asking for this, asking for that?

The other day driving south on Interstate 85, I stopped in at a restaurant, a truck stop where the food is basic, and the servings are generous. While sitting there having a sandwich, I read a sign on the wall, "Some of you think you are not being paid what you are worth — be grateful.''

That's worth thinking about. So intense is our desire for more that we seldom pause to give thanks for what is, and rarely do we think in terms of what we can give because our way is consumed with getting.

I think this is why Christ spoke and taught so often about giving. Only giving can free your heart and mine from greed. You do not have to have a lot to be greedy; some with only a little are the most avaricious of all.

His kingdom is a kingdom where *reaching out is more prevalent than rejection*. His kingdom is always growing and changing. And the growth and the changes come as a result of reaching out to those who need us. Anything alive is always growing, it is changing because of the infusion of new life and vitality. Study the parables of Christ about his kingdom and you will always find growth there. His kingdom is never static, never standing still, it is never rejecting, it is always reaching out.

I love most sports and attend a wide variety of sports events, but I have never been to an auto race. There is nothing appealing to me about watching cars drive around in a circle at terrific speeds, hoping, expecting, that before the day is over there will be a wreck. I see cars going in circles everyday at Lenox Mall, and know the feeling of hoping that someone will leave so I can find a parking spot. I read that when there is some problem on the track that endangers the race drivers, a yellow light is flashed. It is not a signal to slow down, to stop, but a signal for them to hold their places. As they go around the track they are neither to gain or fall back, they must stay in place.[6]

To stay in place is not the strategy of Christ's kingdom. His kingdom is always moving, always reaching, stretching, never rejecting. For the kingdom to thrive it must be always reaching, winning, wooing for Christ. I might add that it must always do this against resistance. There are always those opposing forces that say, ''Let's stand still, let's stay here, let's stay with what we've got." But, the key to life is in reaching. Jesus was right that day of confrontation when he said to Pilate, "My kingdom is not of this world." We shall not see the coming of his kingdom in this life; but in the reaching, in the stretching, in our strivings to attain it here and now, we shall find our highest destiny and our deepest satisfaction. Think about it if you will — the people we love the most are those people who are not stuck on self, but always reaching out for others — those who are serving, not shoving; those who share, rather than grasp. Isn't it true that the persons we admire the most are those who live in faith, rather than react in fear; those persons who seem to march with majesty through life's flux and fury. Isn't it true that we intuitively know that life is found in reaching out, in giving, rather than in getting?

So, when he said, "I am a king," he taught us something. He taught us a deeper lesson than the obvious earthly pomp and power. Ask yourself now this essential question:

Is He My King?

Does he reign in your heart? Read carefully this scene including Jesus and Pilate. When the end of it came there stood Jesus, back ripped to shreds by scourging, crowned with thorns, purple robe on his back, all of it mocking him, and Pilate said, "Here is your king." (John 19:14)

But the mob would have none of it. Scourging was not enough, mocking was not enough, spitting upon him was not enough. The purple robe to mark his kingship was not enough. They said, "Crucify him!" And, the strangest thing of all, the religious leaders said, "We have no king but Caesar." (John 19:15)

Astounding, isn't it? They had abandoned every principle to put him to death, these Jews who had fought, resisted, rebelled, and rejected Rome for the sake of their religion now abandoned their principles to embrace Caesar, so that Jesus could be put to death.

Here is your king. What will you do with him? In the long history of France there was a group of kings called, "The Puppet Kings." They were kings who were not allowed to rule. They had the titles, but not the power. They were paid a kind of ceremonial respect, but no one obeyed them. They were accorded a kind of acclaim but given no authority whatever. Isn't that how many of us treat Christ? We admire him but he has no authority in your life and in mine. We accord him respect, but give him little obedience. We do his thing at church on Sunday, but think of him little during the week in the arenas of reality. Many years ago Dr. Harrison Ray Anderson said these words:

> *Hold up your hearts to God, hold them there until the spirit blows, and the fire glows, and then serve the Lord again as the fire does, with joy and gladness.*

> *You know the difference — a dragging discipleship, or one that leaps; a begrudging stewardship, or one that gladly gives; worship that is tardy and unprepared and cold and disjointed, or worship that glows.*[7]

Lukewarmness or apathy is the deadly spiritual disease of our time.

> *It leads to a contraction of the religious life to the private zone of existence and to a failure of moral nerve in the public arena. Apathy is the loss of ability to feel indignant at the work of evil in our lives and in the lives of others. It is the absence of outrage against injustice. It is the erosion of ability to commit oneself to important causes, to care deeply about other people, and to take risks in the struggle against every form of human bondage.*

It is the deadly sin of indifference, apathy and lukewarmness, and we have it in abundance.

Look at your life, what do you see? Is there pride and ambition rather than humility? Is there getting rather than giving?

Is there a turning inward rather than reaching out? Is there trembling fear rather than faith? It all adds up to spiritual apathy — indifference — going through the motions of faith — the spiritual blahs. Do you remember the day Lucy and Charlie Brown talked about the blahs? Charlie was angry and said to Lucy, "Look, don't tell me I'm a blah. I know I'm blah." Lucy responded, "Well, then there's still hope for you, Charlie Brown. If you recognize this in yourself, then that's the first step up from blahdom."

Is he your king? For him to be king in your heart and mine, we must abdicate. We must let go and let him rule and reign in our hearts. Some have been waiting a lifetime and holding him at arm's length. A woman had lived a wild and wasteful life, no passion was unexpressed, no desire was restrained; but in a transforming moment, Christ changed her and she wrote about it in a pamphlet with this title, "Annie Doesn't Live Here Anymore."[9]

It matters not how or where, but that needs to happen in your life. We need to abdicate so that there can be a coronation, a transforming moment when Christ comes to rule. A contemporary Canadian poet said it very eloquently:

I hear thee and I answer, O my captain,
I will aboard and quickly put to sea,
For where thou art 'tis better than an harbour,
And in the breeze beside thee I am free.[10]

In he your king?

Notes

[1] Benjamin E. Mays, *Disturbed About Man*, (John Knox Press, Richmond, Virginia, 1969), p. 114.

[2] Maxie Dunnam, *Jesus's Claims — Our Promises*, (The Upper Room, Nashville, Tennessee, 1985), p. 73.

[3] George M. Docherty, *I've Seen The Day*, (William B. Eerdmans Publishing Company, Grand Rapids, Michigan, 1984), p. 172.

[4] David S. Belasic and Paul M. Schmidt, *The Penguin Principles,* (The C.S.S. Publishing Company, Lima, Ohio 1986) p. 17.

[5] Kenneth L.Chafin, *I and II Corinthians*, from "The Communicator's Commentary," (Word Books, Waco, Texas, 1985) p. 31.

[6] *Ibid*, p. 95.

[7] Harrison Ray Anderson, *God's Way*, (Fleming H. Revell, Westwood, New Jersey, 1955), p. 147.

[8] From "The Passion of God and the Prophetic Task of Pastoral Ministry" by Daniel L. Migliore in *The Pastor as Prophet*, ed. Earl E. Shelp and Ronald H. Sunderland (New York: The Pilgrim Press, 1985) pp. 116-17.

[9] Dunnam, *Jesus' Claims — Our Promises,* p. 83.

[10] R. B. Y. Scott, "O Voice That Calls To Me," from *Masterpieces of Religious Verse*, ed. by James Dalton Morrison, (Harper and Brothers, New York, 1948), p. 48.

I Am The Way!

Scripture Reading: John 14:1-6
Text: *"I am the way, the truth, and the life: No one comes to the father, but by me." (John 14:6)*

The evening meal was over, Jesus and his disciples were still lingering around the table. The table talk continued, a time of intimate conversation among friends — the waning moments of an evening of great contrasts.

> . . . *It began in the clash of human ambitions. The disciples had seen the acclaim of the people as they entered the city. If a kingdom was being established they wanted to be at the forefront, so they argued, contended with one another as to who would be the greatest in the coming kingdom.*

> . . . *Jesus had quieted the self-assertion among them by taking a towel and filling a servant's role. He washed their feet, cleaning the dirt and dust from their feet, a common courtesy they had overlooked.*

> . . . *The disciples could feel the menace in the air and there was talk of betrayal around the table. It was to their credit that each of the disciples noted that there was a potential betrayer in each of them as they asked, "Lord, is it I?"*

There was the stirring of momentous events in the air. They did not know, as Jesus did, that this would be their last meal, their last time together before he was to suffer and die.
. . . Judas had already left to betray him. (John 13:27-30)
. . . Peter, who loudly proclaimed his capacity to be steadfast, would in a matter of hours deny he ever knew this Jesus of Nazareth. (John 13:37-38)
. . . Soon, when the die was cast and lines were drawn, and the trek to the place of death was eminent, all of them, save

one, would flee for their lives. (John 16:32)

So, they were troubled as they talked around the table, they did not know why, but intuition told them that something was about to happen. Jesus was right on target when he said, "Let not your hearts be troubled," (John 14:1) and talked about his provision, his preparations for them and for us, reminded them that he was the key to the present and the future. Thomas, the disciple who seems so much like many of us, was not satisfied with what seemed to be vague promises. He asserted that he did not understand what it was all about. He did not know fully where Christ was going and since he did not know, how could he possibly know the way? Then Jesus spoke ten words to the eleven troubled men in that borrowed room, "I am the way, the truth, and the life; no man comes to the father but by me." (John 14:6)

William Barclay says that when Jesus said these ten words, he took three of the great claims of the Jewish religion and asserted that they found their full expression in him. What do they mean today? What do they mean to you and to me?

Note that he said:

I Am The Way!

Some months back Sara and I were attending a conference in Orlando, Florida. We had one afternoon free, so we decided to go to Epcot. We did not know the way, though we had been told that our hotel was not very far from it. So I did the best I could, and asked a cab driver in front of the hotel the way. He said to me, "The way to Epcot? Follow me, and I will show you, it's not very far." He not only showed us the way but added some information, "On the way back exit on International Boulevard." That is close to what Christ is saying. He is saying, I am your guide, I will show you the way, I will take you there, I will talk with you while you are going.

Isn't it interesting that one of the most beloved people alive today is a gracious woman who lives in Calcutta, India. She has electrified the world by trying to love those no one else wants to love. Someone once asked Mother Teresa how she lives with, takes the immense problems of Calcutta. She replied, "I focus on the Lord and not the problems. Then I can deal with the problems holding the strong hand of Jesus."[1]

It is a great promise that our Lord is making. He is not only the *way*, but promises to walk with us in our quest, our struggle to get there.

He also said:

I Am The Truth!

You do not live very long until you realize that everyone does not define truth in the same way. To some, truth is what they want to do, when they want to do it, and how they want to do it. The ancient Persians boasted that they taught their boys three things: to ride, to shoot, and to speak the truth. When you combine what the Old Testament says about truth with what the New Testament teaches about truth, you get an appealing picture. You have what can be trusted, what can be depended on, what is stable in a world of reality. Truth does not desert, it never betrays, it can always be counted upon. In a world of flux and change, truth is of immeasurable value. Truth is what really counts in the real world.

You know there are ways of telling the truth without conveying reality, what is real. One of life's little dramas was unfolded between a teacher and one of her pupils. It was a cold day and this kindergarten teacher was helping a little boy get into his snowsuit. It was one of those snowsuits that had snaps and fasteners galore, and in order to get him into the thing, she finally had to get him to lie down on the floor. When finally she had him in the suit, all buttoned and snapped up, they were nose to nose there on the floor, and with a solemn expression he looked up and said, "This isn't my snowsuit." With a grace that was divinely given, she very patiently helped him out of the suit. It was then that he decided to continue his conversation with the teacher by saying, "This is my sister's snowsuit. My mother said I could wear it today."[2]

He had told the truth, all the way, but had not connected it with reality. When Jesus said, I am the *truth* he was saying that he was dependable, a fixed truth in a world of flux. Not only did he teach us the truth, he lived it. He is an example of truth. Truth and character go together in Jesus, and they must go together in us if we are to live in truth. He was proclaiming that he was consistently living what he taught.

We are all measured by truth. Our character reveals what we believe to be true, sometimes we wish that it did not. One of the things Christ expects of us is consistency between character and conduct, between profession and performance.

You would not ask a philanderer to teach a class on fidelity to one's marital vows. The request would not be made to a supreme egotist to discuss the meaning of humility. A non-pledger would not be asked to head the Every Member Canvass (stewardship) effort at the Peachtree Presbyterian Church, nor would he or she be asked to give a public testimony on tithing. A chronic complainer would hardly be asked to discuss the role of joy in the Christian life. A miser could hardly develop a theme on generosity.

Jesus lived what he taught, so must we, if we are to walk in the way of truth.

As the shades of evening gave way to the darkness of night, there was an impending air of menace. Our Lord, seeking to ease the anxiety of those who had shared his life, sought to teach them something, give them something that would stand the test of life for them and for us. He said, I am the way, the truth, and:

I Am The Life!

He wants us to move beyond knowing to living. "I am come that you may have life . . . more abundantly." (John 10:10) This is what he always wants for us, for every person, in every place, in every circumstance. He showed us the way by the way he lived and savored life. His concern was always for others. He was never wrapped up in himself. John Ruskin said something all of us should remember, "When a man is all wrapped up in himself, he makes a pretty small package."

The key to living, as far as Jesus was concerned, was not in self-interest. In his book, *My Creator, My Friend*, Bruce Larson quotes a statement about how we should live. I believe this is a reflection of how Christ wants us to live.

People are unreasonable, illogical and self-centered: Love them anyway.

If you do good, people will accuse you of selfish ulterior motives: do good anyway.

If you're successful, you win false friends and make true enemies: try to succeed anyway.

The good you do today will be forgotten tomorrow: be good anyway.

Honesty and frankness will get you nowhere: They make you vulnerable. Be honest and frank anyway.

People favor underdogs, but they follow the top dogs: Fight for some underdogs anyway.

What you spend days building may be destroyed overnight: Do it anyway.

People really need help but they attack you if you try to help them: Try anyway.

Give the world the best you have and you get kicked in the mouth: give the world the best you have anyway. [3]

The reason many of us do not have "life more abundant"

is because we are trying to find it in the wrong places, the wrong way. I believe Christ wants us to have life in fulness and to face it unafraid. There was a contagious attraction to him, people were drawn to him because there was a zest about the way he lived. He offers all of that to us when he says, "I am the life." The key to life is to be found in the way he lived.

I remember when Dr. Norman Vincent Peale visited our church. At eighty-seven years of age, he had a zest for life, a joy in living that was contagious. I recently read a story about him that illustrates this. A Presbyterian minister was visiting with Dr. Peale in New York when Dr. Peale was only eighty-two. They visited, and then had prayer together. When the prayer time was concluded, the friend said to Dr. Peale, "That was great! Why don't we form a covenant to pray for each other every day wherever we are in the world." Dr. Peale took to the idea with gusto — in fact, he enlarged upon the idea by saying, "Wonderful, let's make it for twenty years." The minister, a little bit startled by the suggestion, said, "But, Norman, you'll be 102 years old then. Dr. Peale replied, "That's right, and I'll need your prayers then more than ever."[4]

I earnestly believe that that is the way Christ wants us to live, to experience the joy of life, and he offers it to you and to me. He offers us the *way* we should walk, and he promises to walk with us.

He offers us the *truth*, a reminder that truth and character go together, that our talk and our walk should be consistent.

He offers us *life*, promising to give us his power as we live, so that we can live more abundantly.

We know what he offers, but there is a requirement placed upon you and upon me. We must *accept* his offer. Did you notice that sentence in the text, "No man comes to the father but by me"? H. G. Wells was very close to this when he wrote in *God the Invisible King*:

> *Religion is the first thing and the last thing, and until a man has found God . . . he begins at no beginning, he works to no end.*"[5]

When I went off to college, I was a candidate for the ministry under care of Harmony Presbytery. As I look back, it was a tremendous advantage for me to know where I was going as my education began. In those days, the Candidate's Committee of Harmony Presbytery received my report card, and it was read publicly before the Presbytery. I can tell you, that is motivation! Once a year I had to appear before the Presbytery in person to give an account of my progress, my plans and studies. In retrospect there is only one thing I remember about those appearances. Mr. Knox, a white-haired minister who was not easy to know, but whose life just conveyed grace and integrity, would get up and ask the same question every time I was there, "Frank, are you making any progress in your walk with Christ?"

That is the question I want to pose to you. Are you making any progress in your walk with Christ? Progress begins with our acceptance of him, when we embrace his offer of grace.

Last year around Easter many people were glued to their television sets for several nights as the mini-series, "The Thorn Birds," was presented. It was a moving story. In some ways it was unfortunate that this program was slated for the early part of Holy Week. Yet, perhaps there was significance, for there is a tie here between this story and our Christian faith.

The story centers around an old Celtic legend about a bird which sings only once in its life. It sings that single song more sweetly than any other creature on the face of the earth. From the moment it leaves its nest, this bird searches for a thorn tree and does not rest until it has found one.

Having found its thorn tree, the bird sings among the tree's savage branches and impales itself on the longest, sharpest spine. Then, dying, it rises above its own agony to out-carol the lark and the nightingale. The whole world stills to listen, and God in his heaven smiles. The best is bought at the cost of great pain, so says the legend.

It was Christmas time in 1939. King George VI of England,

standing on the threshold of war's horror and destruction, reminded his people of a friend they could trust. He quoted this poem:

I said to the man at the gate of the year:

"Give me a light that I might walk safely into the unknown." He replied, "Go forth into the darkness, and put your hand in the hand of God.
That shall be for you better than light, and safer than a known way."
So I went forth, and finding the hand of God, trod gladly into the night.
Then God led me safely toward the hills and the breaking of day in the lone east.[6]

I can promise you that he always leads us toward the light, if we accept him! Come out of whatever darkness that surrounds you, and come to him, where there is light.

Notes

[1] Lloyd J. Ogilvie, *If God Cares, Why Do I Still Have Problems?* (Word Books, Waco, Texas, 1985), p. 133.

[2] Bruce Larson, *My Creator, My Friend*, (Word Books, Waco, Texas, 1986) pp. 54-55.

[3] *Ibid*, pp. 86-87.

[4] Ogilvie, *If God Cares, Why Do I Still Have Problems?*, pp. 128-129.

[5] *If I Had Only One Sermon To Preach*, edited by Dr. Charles Stelze, (Harper and Brothers Publishers, New York, London, 1927), p. 94.

[6] Larson, *My Creator, My Friend*, pp. 106-107.

I Am The Resurrection and The Life!

Scripture Reading: John 11:5-7; 17-27
Text: "I am the resurrection and the life; he who believes in me though he die, yet shall he live." (John 11:25)

Lazarus was sick unto death and his sisters sent for Jesus. The tone of the passage would indicate that there was a very close relationship between Jesus, Mary, Martha, and their bother, Lazarus. They lived in Bethany, about two miles from Jerusalem, and it would be reasonable to assume that over the years, when Jesus was in Jerusalem, he probably visited them frequently. Lazarus was now critically ill and his sisters sent word to Jesus asking him to come.

They wanted him to come for two reasons:

1. When there is a crisis, either of illness, death, or circumstances, there is a need for support and comfort from those who care, who love you the most.
2. They knew that Jesus had special powers to heal and to restore.

Jesus decided immediately that he would go to them, but he delayed going for two days; there was tension among his disciples about his going to Jerusalem. There was danger in the city. When he finally arrived, his friend was dead, and had been buried for four days.

The record goes to great lengths to show that Lazarus was dead. Jesus told his disciples before he even began the journey that Lazarus was already dead. (John 11:11) The stone was in place across the entrance to the tomb. (John 11:38) The corpse had been rolled in the burial bandages, actually called "traveling dress." (John 11:44) The traditional mourners were there, wailing in sorrow. (John 11:28) Martha warned Jesus that, if the stone were removed from the entrance to the tomb, the odor would be bad, for decay of the earthly remains undoubtedly had begun. (John 11:39)

The picture is exquisitely and meticulously clear. Lazarus was dead, totally in the grip of death. Jesus called him forth from the tomb, back from death to life. (John 11:43) This was the setting, the context in which Jesus made his great claim:

I am the resurrection and the life; he who believes in me, though he die, yet shall he live, and whoever lives and believes in me shall never die. (John 11:25)

What a claim! What a statement! As we study this great claim, I will build my thoughts around three words. The first word is:

Promise!

"I am the resurrection and the life."

Jesus is saying here that our future is not to be found in the correctness of our creed, in sterile doctrine, nor rigid rules, but that the key is confidence in a person, the person of Jesus Christ. It was a pattern of his teachings. You remember that he said:

Abandon your darkness because "I am the light of the world."

Wander aimlessly no more for I will care for you for "I am the good shepherd."

Enter into the more abundant life that I have promised you for "I am the door."

Forget about suffering spiritual malnutrition for "I am the bread of life."

Give me the direction of your life for "I am a king."

Embrace the nourishing, vital connection that sustains and replenishes for "I am the vine, you are the branches."

Accept the completeness available to you as you struggle between already and not yet for "I am alpha and omega."

Walk with me and you will be empowered in this life and given safe haven in the life to come for "I am the way, the truth, and the life."

Again, again, and again he says, have confidence in me. Our faith is centered in a person, and in the gravest crisis of them all, the crisis of death, he says, believe in me, have confidence in me for "I am the *resurrection* and the *life*."

He makes his claims. He gives these promises based on his capacity to keep them. Our confidence is in him.

It is not merely a promise of new life in the face of death, but it is the promise of new life now, here, every day. There are many people who long for, pray for, hope for a new beginning — a new start — new strength — new resources.

There are businessmen and women caught up in the arena of commerce, where pressures abound, temptations are plentiful. Their days are days of endless transactions, quotas to be met, deals to be made; their nights are restless with the disturbing question, "What does it all mean?" "To what end is all of this striving?" "Is there some larger connection I am missing?" Let me tell you that because He lives he can and he will breath new life, new purpose in all of your business dealings.

There are men and women today who have crossed the Rubicon between right and wrong. You have not kept your promises, nor lived up to your promise. But Christ can resurrect you, and give you new order and peace in your life today.

Some of you are caught in habits that control you. You cannot control them, and you need help. Christ can make you new, not tomorrow, but today.

There are those who live not in colors of bright blue, but dull gray — each day duller than the day before. What does the resurrection offer us? It offers us new life, not in the by and by, but *now*! While listening to the radio I heard the words of a song and recall them thus:

If I built this fortress around your heart —
Encircled you with trenches and barbed wire
Then let me build a bridge
For I cannot fill the chasm
And let me set the battlements on fire.

The *resurrection* that Christ offers begins now, helping us to build bridges and tear down walls, and to "set the battlements on fire." Let me share with you a line or two written by my daughter, Vicki, who is a student at Princeton Theological Seminary, Princeton, New Jersey:

> *Our lives lie waiting for the breath of God to raise them — and so do our relationships with others. Anger or neglect have replaced love and caring too often in our relationships with spouses, parents, children, siblings, friends and co-workers.* [1]

The resurrecting "breath of God" is available now, it can begin now!

The second word we need to look at is:

Response!

"I am the resurrection and the life, he who believes in me." (John 11:25)

Resurrection is available to all who believe. We have to respond. Phillips Brooks, the great Boston preacher said:

> *The great Easter truth is not that we are to live newly after death, but that we are to be new here and now by the power of the resurrection.*

That is true — but only if you respond, only if you believe. A comtemporary writer has created a fictitious conversation between the writer and some of the followers of Jesus after his crucifixion:

> *"Why are you so downhearted, Peter."*
> *"Jesus is dead," he answers.*
> *"Well, James, why are you so glum?"*
> *"Jesus is dead."*

*"And you, John, what has gone wrong with you? Where
is your old spark?"*
"Jesus is dead."

*The questioner inquiring about their plans for the future said,
"Well then, Peter, what are you going to do with your life
from now on?"*
"Go back to my boat and start fishing again, I guess."

*"And you, James and John, what is in store for you now
that Jesus is dead?"*
"Back to mending nets."[2]

Isn't that familar to you? We celebrate Easter, the trumpets sound, the songs are sung, the moment brings tears to our eyes, and a sense of joy in our hearts; and then, it is back to more of the same — nothing has really happened. If we really believe that he lives, we have to respond to the resurrection.

When the disciples heard the incredible news that he was alive, they responded to it, and what a response it was. The denier, Peter, became a champion for Christ. The doubter, Thomas, became a believer. Those who fled the city became brave and bold. They even had a larger view of things.

It is easier to say that it is necessary to respond than it is to respond, because faith and belief collide with circumstances daily in your life and mine. It is hard to give any of the control, the management of our life over to Christ.

During the past year we have witnessed an unparalleled series of air disasters. Weather related crashes, terroristic acts, mechanical failures, all combined to take a terrible toll in human lives. The other night, I flew to Philadelphia for a board meeting, on a stretch DC-8. It was jammed with people, and it set me to thinking. Imagine, if you would, that you are the pilot of a stretch DC-8. It is eight o'clock in the evening, and you have been flying with Delta for twenty years. The plane is returning to Atlanta from Philadelphia, and you have been flying in severe weather all the way. You have been cleared for landing at Hartsfield and it is an instrument landing. There are more than 200 people aboard the plane. As you make the final approach, you are hearing two voices in your headset. One is from the Air Traffic Controller speaking with an awareness of a great deal of information. Electronic devices surround the Controller. He sees other planes on the radar screen. The sole purpose of the Controller is to guide you in for a safe landing. The instructions you are being given as pilot are consistent with what the instruments on board your plane are telling you. In other words, the information is confirmed.

But, there is a second voice you are hearing. It is the voice of intuition, your sight, your senses. You gaze out through the blinding rain, you strain to catch a glimpse of the runway lights. Your sense of the matter is that you are drifting to the right, that the nose of the plane is too low. You want to correct things a bit, but the voice from the tower is saying, "Steady now, you're doing fine. Your flight path is perfect; just hold it there."

A moment of decision has arrived. Do you believe the Air Traffic Controller — do you respond to that belief — or do you rely on those intuitions? Will you trust the voice that has greater access to information, greater knowledge than you have? The safety of more than 200 passengers hangs in the balance. My hope is that the pilot would obey the voice from the tower, that the pilot would respond to the promise of safe landing.[3]

This is not a perfect illustration, but it is close to what I am trying to convey. It is not enough to get the information about the resurrection promise of Christ. We need to respond, to believe. I like some words that Annie Johnson Flint wrote:

I have faith in him, not in my faith
That may fail, tomorrow or today;
Trust may weaken, feeling pass away,
Thoughts grow weary, anxious, or depressed;
I believe in God — and here I rest.[4]

We must respond to what we believe. Whittier said,

When in the maddening maze of things,
And tossed by storms and flood,
To one fixed trust my spirit clings,
I know that God is good.

In all of life's flux and fury, in chance and changes, we have a choice — to respond.

Our Lord promised us something, and we have to respond to that promise. Beyond *promise* and *response* there is the word:

Redemption!

"He who believes in me, though he dies, yet shall he live." (John 11:25)

"Yet shall he live" — redeemed, made alive, made new. It is our privilege to be able to believe, in the darkest of times, that light is more powerful than darkness. It is our privilege to believe, that in the bleakness of pain and suffering, hope is stronger than all our pain, and that there beats at the heart of all that is a redemptive purpose in Jesus Christ. It is our privilege to believe that, even when we are falling, failing, there is a lifting power to bring us to our feet. The last words of Edward, the confessor, were:

Weep not, I shall not die; and as I leave the land of the dying,
I trust to see the blessings of the Lord in the land of the
living. [5]

It is this precious promise, this redeeming impulse that runs through life; our heads cannot grasp it, but our intuition knows that it is true. This affirmation of the heart gives us strength to continue, to hope, to believe. I flew to Charleston recently to see a friend who is struggling with illness. Her little grandson, who was three years old, had died. He was a joy to his grandmother and grandfather, and to his mother and father. I had splashed with him in a swimming pool last summer. Suddenly, a few weeks ago, he collapsed and died. In the aftermath of his passing, his mother wrote these words:

Morning kisses, small armed love,
Taken to join our Father above,
Missed by each life that he touched
Daniel West Fraser whose heart shared so much.
Gathered together, we feel as we pray
For this young child each precious day.
Comfort us, Lord, as you open heaven's door.
To our broken hearts faith restore.
Bless our memories, please fill them with joy,
Though his time on earth was brief,
Every day we'll cherish our boy.[6]

Gone to be sure, it wrenches the heart, but remember the words of Jesus, "yet shall he live." Words cannot describe it, minds cannot comprehend it, but there rises in the human spirit the desire to respond to a larger reality than we are surrounded with here. It was the claim of all claims, the promise of all promises. It is the promise that sets us free.

Because of this promise of new life:

We Are Victors, Not Victims!

Browning wrote,

. . . if this be all . . . and other life awaits us not . . . for one I say, "Tis a poor cheat, a stupid bungle, a wretched failure." I, for one, protest against it, I hurl it back with scorn.[7]

Those words do not apply to us — we are victors, not victims. As I stand by an open grave, looking into the faces of a grieving family, I often quote these words:

*And God will wipe away every tear from their eyes; there
shall be no more death, nor sorrow, nor crying: and there
shall be no more pain, for the former things have passed
away. (Revelation 21:4)*

And with confidence I can say, "Death you have lost your
sting! Grave you have no victory here. You do not, you cannot, speak the final word today."
Yes, we are victors, not victims.

> *Dear Lord, How shall we know that they
> Still walk unseen with us and thee,
> Nor sleep, nor wander far away?"
> He smiled: "Abide in me.*[8]

Victor Hugo said it so well:

*When I go down to my grave, I can say I have finished my
day's work, but I cannot say that I have finished my life.
My day's work will begin again the next morning. The tomb
is not a blind alley, it is a thoroughfare. It closes in the
twilight to open in dawn.*[9]

In the story of Zorba the Greek, a man invests all his money
in a risky venture — an unproven way of getting timber down
the mountain. The community needs the wood to reinforce
the walls of an old mine, and if they can get the mine going
again full employment and prosperity will return to the village.
On the day the logs are to be placed on the unproven slide,
the whole village turns out. They are filled with hope, hope
which soon turns to despair. The slide collapses. His invest-
ment lost, the man contemplates leaving the village.
Zorba speaks to him, "Boss man, I've never loved a man
as I love you, but there's one thing you lack — the little madness to be free."
Zorba, who is standing beside the pile of rubble, begins
to laugh. The man who has lost his money says, "Why are
you laughing?" Through his laughter, Zorba says, "Have you

ever seen a more stupendous crash?'' The man captures the spirit of the moment and asks, ''Zorba, will you teach me to dance?'' The story ends with these two men dancing, celebrating life at the site of their greatest failure.[10]

We all need a "little madness to be free," so that we can be victors, instead of victims, so that we can be liberated from the goal of perpetual success, so that we can learn how to dance.

Kipling reminds us that we reach maturity when we can, "meet with truth and disaster and treat those two imposters just the same." We must have something in life that is bigger than both. Christ is alive, and that gives us the madness to be free.

We also can live with:

Visions of Hope, Not Despair!

William J. and Gloria Gaither have written a beautiful contemporary hymn which includes these words:

Because he lives I can face tomorrow;
Because he lives all fear is gone;
Because I know he holds the future,
And life is worth the living just because he lives.[11]

We live with hope, not despair. Eda Leshan, in *Learning to Say Goodbye*, tells of visiting a friend who had lost her husband. They went out to the cemetery together, and stood there by his grave and reminisced a bit. They fell silent into their memories; words seemed so inadequate for the moment. Then a child of the deceased did something amazing — she ran and did cartwheels over her father's grave. Eda Lesham was surprised, but the mother of the child said, "Liz hasn't done any cartwheels since Bob died. He used to love it when she did."

And upon reflection Eda Leshan wrote:

*I tried to understand just what Liz's message to her father
meant. Then I realized that her gift to him was to pick up
the threads of her life and begin to live as fully as she could.
The time comes to begin to do cartwheels again, to express
our joy in being alive.*[12]

We live in hope — not despair. Where there is no faith in
the future, there is no power in the present. Studdert Kennedy
knew what he was talking about when he said, "If Jesus died,
naught but the winter and gloom remain."

But, *he did not die.* And this reality changes everything
for you, for me, for now, for eternity.

Hope for the Christian is not wishful thinking, it is the very
substance of faith.

Eric Sloane, a noted artist, published his autobiography
under the title, *Eighty: An American Souvenir.* In the book,
he reprinted an etching of a tombstone, which bore these
words, "God knows I tried."[13]

An attractive young woman, intelligent, wealthy, and beautiful, drove her silver Mercedes convertible to a hotel. She had
everything, it seemed. She had amassed a fortune through
timely investments. She checked into the hotel, and then
checked out for good. She died of a drug overdose and left
a note that read, "I'm tired of clapping with one hand."[14]

You need to keep on trying, keep on keeping on, don't ever
give in. God knows you are trying. And because he lives, the
applause never stops, no one has to clap with one hand anymore. We live in hope, not despair.

Jiro Ishli, after the destruction of Hiroshima, entered the
city to search in vain for his parents. His heart was heavy as
he left that place of death and destruction. There were no
blooming flowers, no gentle breeze waving the leaves of any
tree, just the stillness and silence of death. On the way out
of the city, his eyes caught a bit of green. At the roots of a
burned tree was a small shoot of green, of life.[15] He knew then
that death could not and had not won — that life has in it
the impulse of victory. That is what Easter means.

I cannot explain what happened, but I know it is true, that things changed forever between Good Friday and Easter Sunday. There was agony on Friday, glory on Sunday. There was death on Friday, life on Sunday. There were evil winds on Friday, good triumphs on Sunday. A dead body enclosed in a tomb on Friday, a living Lord on Sunday. Despair on Friday, hope on Sunday. Darkness on Friday, and the trembling of the earth, lights and shouts of joy on Sunday. Never again, never again do we live without hope.

> *They thought that death would silence Him,*
> *They nailed Him to a tree.*
> *But I am sure He rose again,*
> *Because He lives in me!*

> *I never envy those who hear Him*
> *Preach in Galilee,*
> *For since my heart has turned to Him,*
> *He daily walks with me.*

> *They thought that death would conquer Him,*
> *They nailed Him to a tree.*
> *I know, I know He conquered death,*
> *Because He lives in me.*
>   *(Anonymous)*

He will live in you — if you will let him.

Notes

1 From a Sermon on Ezekiel 37:1-4, p. 1, Vicki Harrington Franch.

2 Dr. Frank H. Seilhamer, *Adventures In Faith*, (New World Press, York, Pennsylvania, 1982), p. 62.

3 Arnold Prater, *How To Be Happy In An Unhappy World*, (Thomas Nelson Publishers, Nashville, Tennessee, 1983), pp. 75-76.

4 Poem by Annie Johnson Flint used by permission of Evangelical Publishers, a Division of Scripture Press Publication, Limited.

5 William Barclay, *The Gospel of John*, Volume 2, (Westminster Press, Philadelphia, 1955), p. 110.

6 "Our Boy," by Mary Edna Fraser (written on the death of her three year old son.)

7 *The Speaker's Bible, The First Epistle to the Corinthians*, edited by the Reverend James Hastings, D.D., (Baker Book House, Grand Rapids, Michigan, 1962), p. 140.

8 *The Speaker's Bible, The Gospel According to St. John*, Volume, II, edited by the Reverend Edward Hastings, M.A., (Baker Book House, Grand Rapids, Michigan, 1962), p. 25.

9 *The Speaker's Bible, 1 Corinthians*, Volume 11, p. 139.

10 "Pulpit Digest," September/October, 1985, from Sermon, "This Thing Called Life," by Rabbi Edward Paul Cohn, Temple Saini, Pittsburg, PA., pp. 38-39.

11 "Because He Lives." Words and music by William J. and Gloria Gaither. © 1971 and 1979 by Gaither Music Company. All rights reserved. International copyright secured. Used by permission.

12 *Ibid*, p. 88-89.

13 Robert Schuller, *The Be (Happy) Attitudes*, (Word Books, Waco, Texas, 1985), p. 174-176.

14 Dunnam, *Jesus's Claims — Our Promises*, pp.97-98.

15 Garnett M. Wilder, *Using Your Emotions Creatively*, (Judson Press, Valley Forge, Pennsylvania, 1984), p. 28. Used by permission of Judson Press.